Harzfelds™

A Brief History

JOE & MICHELE BOECKHOLT

THE
History
PRESS

Published by The History Press
Charleston, SC 29403
www.historypress.net

Front cover illustration from a direct mail brochure, circa 1949.
All images from the authors' collection unless otherwise noted.

First published 2009
Second printing 2010

Manufactured in the United States

ISBN 978.1.59629.733.3

Library of Congress Cataloging-in-Publication Data
Boeckholt, Joe.
Harzfeld's : a brief history / Joe and Michele Boeckholt.
p. cm.
Includes bibliographical references.
ISBN 978-1-59629-733-3
1. Harzfeld's (Firm) 2. Harzfeld's (Firm)--History. 3. Department stores--Missouri--
Kansas City--History. 4. Kansas City (Mo.)--History. I. Boeckholt, Michele. II. Title.
HF5465.U6H37 2009
381'.14109778411--dc22
2009045617

Notice: The information in this book is true and complete to the best of our knowledge. It
is offered without guarantee on the part of the author or The History Press. The author
and The History Press disclaim all liability in connection with the use of this book.

Dedicated to the late
Erasmus "Ras" Beall
*whose myriad design talents
inspire us*

and

Patricia George
*A model creative spirit
for the enjoyment of life*

Contents

Preface

We take pleasure in collecting historical ephemera of the Kansas City area. While attending a flea market at the American Royal complex in the mid-'90s, we came upon photos, illustrations and printed materials originally from the estate of Harzfeld's longtime display director, Erasmus "Ras" Beall. Realizing that these items told an interesting story as a group, the gracious dealer offered the lot for a reasonable price. It was at that particular point in time that our affinity for the Harzfeld's specialty store was born. Since then, this project has found us, through friends, store associates, fashionistas and historians. This personal project has been the perfect intersection of art, design, fashion and Kansas City history.

Arriving in Kansas City years after Harzfeld's was no longer in existence, we have thoroughly enjoyed meeting the amazing people associated with the store and hearing their nostalgic memories from an era that's passed. While building our knowledge of the store, we were gifted a collection of original illustrations from the Historic Garment District of Kansas City. We have been honored to be caretakers of these works and are cataloging and organizing all Harzfeld's material, exploring ways for these items to be preserved and shared with those who yearn for an earlier time.

Acknowledgements

W e would like to thank the many individuals and organizations that have assisted us with our research over the past several years. Without their help, this project would not have been possible. Our sincere apologies to those we've forgotten, were unable to follow up with further or are not represented in this publication. You are invited to share your remembrances of the store through our blog via harzfelds.com. This will allow us to share stories of individuals and departments not properly covered in our book. We intend to continue documenting the history of Harzfeld's in an effort to create a more complete archive.

A very special thank-you to Lester Siegel Jr. for his sharing of the past. A written history that he documented was a catalyst for this book, and we appreciate his time and memories.

Janet and Frank Altmann
Dave Bales
Danny Bergman
Ann Brownfield
John G. Cate
Warren Dalton
Kathy Drew
Suzanne Dryer
Leesa Fanning
Helen Farnsworth

Katherine Frohoff
Patricia George
Sheryl Hagadorn
Jan Sokoloff Harness
Lloyd Hellman
Wendy Hodgden
Mary Hodgins
Paula Holmquist
David W. Jackson
Arthur III and Karon Kabrick

ACKNOWLEDGEMENTS

Gary and Elaine Kabrick
Saul Kass
Mary Jane Krugh
Judy Lanes
Linda Louis
Dale Lundhigh
Terence O'Malley
JoLynne (Walz) Martinez
Richard McOsker
Cliffton "Mac" McWaid
Melissa Miller
Penny Montgomery
Denise Morrison
Heather Paxton
Connie Ramos
Jack Rees

Lorene Roberson
Beth Robinson
Jan Schall
John and Kim Schinkel
Dan Schrock
Lisa Shockley
Lester Siegel Jr.
Jonathan Simcosky
Steve Sitton
Dave Spivey
Dr. Deborah Stephens
Drolette (Bradley) Weideman
Donna Welsh
Marc F. Wilson
Holly Wright
LuWayne Yougans

ORGANIZATIONS

The Harry S. Truman Library & Museum
The Historic Garment District Museum of Kansas City
The Independent, Kansas City's Weekly Journal of Society
Jackson County Historical Society
Johnson County Library
Kansas City Public Library
Missouri Valley Special Collections
The Nelson-Atkins Museum of Art
The Thomas Hart Benton Home and Studio State Historic Site
Tulsa City-County Library
Western Historical Manuscripts

Chapter 1

The Beginning

The first ad for the Parisian Cloak Company announced its February 25, 1891 grand opening with the proclamation of "A Card!" It was a card that Ferdinand Siegel was willing to play. He was betting on the future of a young man with ambition. Siegmund Harzfeld proposed to Mr. Siegel a new concept, a specialty store devoted exclusively to women's ready-to-wear to be opened in Kansas City.

Although the meaning of the phrase may be lost to us today, hundreds of ladies understood "a card" as an invitation and attended, each receiving a floral bouquet as a souvenir. The store at 1108 and 1110 Main Street was lavishly decorated with flowers and plants. Ten salespeople were available to tend to their needs.[1] The women of Kansas City no longer needed to spend time at long appointments with a dressmaker to maintain a fashionable appearance. Up to this time, everything of elegance was custom-tailored. This new merchandising theory, that ladies' ready-made clothing could dress a woman as elegantly as a dressmaker, was a founding principle of the Parisian.[2]

Below is an account from the *Kansas City Globe* as it read the day after the grand opening:

> *The announcement of a spring opening special or clearing sale generally attracts the ladies, but when a new store is thrown open to the public there is enough mystery connected with it to prove too strong an attraction for one of the fair sex to resist. Such was the case yesterday when the doors of the large salesroom, 1108 and 1110 Main Street, were thrown open to the public.*

A CARD!

THE

PARISIAN CLOAK CO.

Of Kansas City will open on **WEDNESDAY, THE 25TH INST.**, with a full line of Foreign and Domestic Novel-in **LADIES', MISSES' AND CHILDREN'S SPRING GARMENTS.**

PARISIAN CLOAK COMP'Y.

Largest Exclusive Cloak House in the West,

1108 AND 1110 MAIN STREET.

The first print ad for the Parisian Cloak Company, announcing its formal opening on Wednesday, February 25; from the four-page *Kansas City Star*, Monday, February 23, 1891.

Carriages were before the entrance all the afternoon, and the visitors were amply repaid for braving the unpleasant weather by the bewildering array of ladies' and children's ready-made garments displayed by the Parisian Cloak Company. On entering the doors, after admiring the magnificent window display of dresses and cloaks, over which were wide spreading palms, the ladies were received by courteous attendants and presented with floral souvenirs, then escorted through the large room, with its pier glasses (mirrors), display cases and racks on which hung cloaks, walking jackets, house jackets and gowns of all descriptions. It was one of the largest and most varied lines of imported and domestic-made garments ever shown in Kansas City, and was praised highly by the visitors.

A generation earlier, in 1842, Albert Harzfeld came to America from Bremen in northern Germany. He was a traveling salesman in Buffalo, New York, where his wife, Caroline, gave birth to their first son, Siegmund, in October 1868.[3] The family moved to Chicago, where Albert partnered with his brother Edward and other Jewish businessmen to manufacture garments. A firm, established in 1880, was successful and employed between eighty and one hundred men and women. However, the combination of allowing customers to purchase on credit and a lack of capital eventually caused problems, and the firm closed in 1884.[4] Soon after, Albert reestablished himself in the garment industry and associated himself with F. Siegel & Brothers, the first wholesale manufacturer of women's ready-to-wear in the United States. In 1887, Albert developed a tumor on his neck. He checked with doctors as the condition progressed and was told he would not survive surgery. The physical pain and stress from the situation eventually led to him taking his own life in May 1890.[5]

Siegmund, often referred to as Sieg, thought of becoming a lawyer, but changed his mind and, as his father had done, went to work for F. Siegel & Brothers. He proposed opening a store in Kansas City, catering exclusively to women. Ferdinand Siegel agreed to finance the store. After the tragic loss of his father, he was most likely looking for a new start. Sieg first helped establish a store in St. Louis and then went on to his chosen destination of Kansas City to make his business venture, which started on the street-level floor at 1110 Main Street on November 4, 1890, a few months prior to the grand opening.

Sieg saw opportunity in Kansas City, a growing community that in decades prior had struggled to establish its place on the trails west. The Chouteau family, early prominent settlers of St. Louis, had exclusive rights to trade with Native Americans in the Missouri River Valley. François and Berenice Chouteau settled in the area by the river in 1821. They established trade with the Indians and trappers, sending their pelts back East. In 1826, their cabin was washed away by a flood, and they moved their trading post farther in from the Missouri River. A half mile south, the area that would later be occupied by the Parisian was a grove of oak trees.[6] As the years passed, various tribes of Indians were forced from their lands and moved

These individual panels were used as decoration in the "Younger Set" shop. The historical motifs of the Indian trader, the early 1900s Parisian Cloak Company storefront and rooster may have been seen as nostalgic during the time of Kansas City's centennial celebration in 1950. They were created by the Harzfeld's display department. Mixed media on plywood, each approximately thirty-six inches in height. *From the estate of Saul Kass (1915–2005), longtime executive for Harzfeld's, starting in 1944.*

west through Kansas City and Westport. The funds they were paid to relocate fed the early economy of the area. As more white settlers moved in, the Native Americans were eventually forced out, moving farther west into progressively restricted areas.[7]

The Civil War brought devastating conflict to Kansas City. It was a time when much of the trade was diverted to other areas. After the war, Kansas City, with a population of about 32,000, had railroad lines coming in from the East. It won out as the passage west with the 1869 opening of the Hannibal Bridge, which provided easier access over the volatile Missouri River. The 1880s saw a real estate boom, but by 1890, with a population of

1110 Main Street, Kansas City, Missouri, circa 1890. From *'Mongst Us* (a revival of an earlier company newsletter by the same name, published by the Harzfeld's credit union) 1, no. 2, November 1940. Many references are made to 1108 as the first storefront; however, this photo suggests that it started at 1110.

1108–1110 Main Street, Kansas City, Missouri, circa 1891. From *'Mongst Us* (revival) 1, no. 2, November 1940.

Parisian Cloak Co.

1108-1110 MAIN STREET.

The Parisian Has Another Big Treat in Store

for Skirt and Waist Buyers

Next Week. All Kinds and All Styles.

..... SPECIALS .....

White waists with embroidered insertions from............... 98c to $5

Pique skirts with embroidered insertion from................ 98c to $10

This little ad was the first of thousands of ads, along with sponsored covers, for the Kansas City society magazine *The Independent. Courtesy of* The Independent, *June 17, 1899.*

133,000, there were a number of empty storefronts and Kansas City was struggling from a depressed economy, which was echoed nationally.

By 1890, individuals with vision and ambition, such as Sieg, saw opportunity. In speaking of the first year, he once said, "We had a little business for two months, then starved the next ten!"[8] There may have been a lean start, but with confidence, he expanded the store to include the second storefront before the grand opening event in February 1891. The store initially offered coats, waists (blouses), petticoats and furs. Promotion through advertising in regional newspapers and the offer of a free illustrated catalogue by mail bolstered the store's growth.

Sieg married twenty-one-year-old Florence Stern on February 7, 1894. She was born in New Orleans, and her family moved to Kansas City in 1885. The couple's honeymoon of several weeks first took them to New Orleans and then on to New York. They returned to Kansas City, where they stayed at the Coates House Hotel on Quality Hill at 1005 Broadway, until they settled in an apartment on Locust, south of Thirteenth Street.[9] Sieg would return to New York twice a year to buy spring and fall fashions for Kansas City.

The Parisian grew along with Kansas City and, in 1897, expanded upward to lease the second floor. The city was perceived as a cow town with its eight packing plants, but a great deal of pride could be taken in this achievement. Agriculture was a large part of the local economy that supported other businesses as they established themselves at the turn of the twentieth century. Kansas City was ready to take the national spotlight by hosting the Democratic National Convention in July 1900, but only three months prior to the event, fire destroyed the newly constructed convention hall, located just five blocks from the Parisian. Kansas Citians pulled together and rebuilt the hall at Thirteenth and Central in time to host the convention.

Left: Heraldic-type shield with "H," as seen in the center of six panels on image below. *Collection of Gary and Elaine Kabrick.*

Below: 1108–1110 Main Street, Kansas City, Missouri, circa 1906. From *'Mongst Us* (revival) 1, no. 2, November 1940.

This amazing achievement gave the city a great sense of community and helped it in addressing challenges to come.

One of those challenges came just three years later, in May 1903. A flood devastated the West Bottoms, destroying homes and businesses. It impaired both sides of the state line, and thousands were left homeless. After the waters receded, the communities rebuilt, with a new-found respect for the power of the rivers. The same waters that granted access to the West and helped attract people to the area then, continue to cause periodic flooding

Looking north on Main. Painted message on south façade of the Parisian. Detail from a period postcard.

today. Efforts to tame the rivers later became a theme illustrated by the store and had direct effects on the business.

In 1906, the store expanded to all five floors of the building, occupying 31,250 square feet of floor space. Improvements costing $50,000 were made, including a new exterior modeled after a Parisian store. There were three new display windows and two entrances. Inside, there were new fixtures of

Above: Looking north on Main, post-1906. The Parisian is on the far left. From a booklet called *Scenes from Kansas City*.

Left: Parisian Cloak Company advertisement, *Kansas City Star*, May 23, 1903.

Harzfeld's display cabinet with "H"s carved on cabriole legs, 42" H x 8'4" W x 28" D.

mahogany, elaborately frescoed walls and new carpets. Two new elevators were installed. Sieg stated, "Since we have the only store of the kind in the West, we felt that we might be pardoned in attempting something individual and distinctive."[10] One of the ways the façade was made more distinctive was by adding heraldic-type shields with "H" insignias, repeated on panels that adorned the second floor. This branding was an early transition in a name change and reflected the pride that Sieg and Florence had in the success of the store.

Chapter 2

Don't Take Life Too Seriously

Don't take life too seriously if you want to get the most out of it. When I went to work it was to make my place in the world so that I could live in it.
—*Siegmund Harzfeld*[11]

Sieg had a number of passions that fulfilled his desire "to work to live." He sponsored a baseball team by the name of, what else, the Parisian Cloak Companys in the City Junior League. Other teams in their league were the Garfields, Bell Telephone Companys, Hyde Parks, C.L. Richmonds, Elmhursts, Olive Athletics and Linwoods (replacing the Warf Rats). There were dozens of amateur teams, including the Coca-Colas, Montgomery Wards, Penn Valley Parks, Kansas City Arts, Sunflowers, Paseo Blues, Rockhill Blues, Baby Elephants, Troost Avenue Athletics, Hoo-hoo Hitters and the Justrites.[12]

When Sieg's friend Louis Stengel bragged to him about his son Charley's sporting ability, he was drafted into "the Parisians" as early as 1907. Years prior, Sieg may have seen the young Charley spraying water on the dirt streets of Kansas City. It was a practice of the day for retailers such as the Parisian to contract with individuals to spray down dirt streets with water to help control the clouds of dust kicked up by horses, wagons and foot traffic. Louis was in charge of arranging these contracts. Charley tried his hand at sprinkling, but he had other ambitions, such as picking up a game of baseball in open lots around town or taking in a vaudeville show. Charley later attended Central High School, just blocks east of Harzfeld's. Sieg paid him, as he did all the players, $1.50 per game. This was Stengel's first taste of "professional" ball.[13]

Years later, he was drafted by the Brooklyn Dodgers while playing minor league ball in Montgomery, Alabama. Charley was given the name "Casey" in honor of his hometown. He went on to play Major League ball with the L.A. Dodgers, Pittsburgh Pirates, Philadelphia Phillies, New York Giants and Boston Braves. He played in three World Series, but his greatest success came later as a manager. Casey led the New York Yankees to win ten pennants in twelve years.

There comes a time in every man's life, and I've had plenty of them.
—*Casey Stengel*

In 1955, Casey returned to Kansas City while managing the Yankees against Kansas City's new entry into the Major Leagues, the Athletics, or A's. Stengel's stylish wife, Edna, was presented with a bottle of French perfume from Harzfeld's in honor of his early relationship with the Kansas City specialty store.[14]

Harzfeld's continued the tradition of team-building by organizing employee bowling, basketball and baseball teams. Sieg's personal and professional behavior set a strong example for his loyal employees, and many individuals and groups within the organization met the bar of civic responsibility.

Another opportunity Sieg found to "live" was through music. Sieg and Florence helped a number of local musicians find their start, including soprano Marion Talley.[15] In 1926, at the age of nineteen, she was the youngest prima donna in New York Metropolitan Opera history. Talley was also supported by Sieg's younger brother Jacob, a prominent Kansas City lawyer.

The store would sell tickets to concerts, sometimes in conjunction with the J.W. Jenkins' Sons music store, as they did in 1915 for a "pop" (popular orchestral) concert at the Convention Hall.[16] The Kansas City Symphony Orchestra Association, which eventually resulted in the establishment of the Kansas City Philharmonic, was a large philanthropic focus for the Harzfelds. Sieg served as president of the association and, in 1929, organized a campaign to sell tickets to a series of four concerts featuring the St. Louis Symphony Orchestra. About 150 women, many of them trained sales staff from Harzfeld's and other stores, went into the community to ask for support of the concert. The years of fundraising and publicity resulted in the Kansas

City Philharmonic's inaugural concert, conducted by Karl Krueger, in December 1933. Free concerts for children, started in 1922, were ensured for many years through the Harzfelds' support. Florence also collected an extensive record library.

The Harzfelds' love of music was nearly rivaled by their love of travel. Sometimes they would retrace the path of their honeymoon. In the summer of 1909, they took a three-month trip to Europe, where they logged 4,000 miles driving through Germany and France, two fashion hubs of the era. By 1931, they had made thirty-seven trips abroad, totaling 400,000 miles. It was said that before he left on a trip, Sieg expressed his farewell good wishes to all employees as they exited the store at closing time.[17] Sieg stated that they never tired of their voyages.

He was also passionate about his commitment to Kansas City and its future, demonstrating civic leadership and pride in many areas, including serving on the Chamber of Commerce and the Merchants' Association. Employee efforts created their own circles of philanthropy, benefitting many local charities.

Always a savvy businessman but willing to take risks, Sieg tried something new in March 1911. Passions carried over to an unconventional approach to business when the Parisian staged a street performance to introduce a new daring fashion. Five young women paraded from the store to the streets in the proposed new trend, harem pants. These pants were only a slight step in liberating women from the long dresses with petticoats. Unless the women were "striding along," the panel, dropping almost to the ankle, was not detected.

The ribbon border was often incorporated in advertisements into the 1920s. *Courtesy of* The Independent, *circa 1910.*

In September 1913, Kansas City held its own "fashion week." National and local models were in full form in several of the downtown stores, both on the runway and in display windows. New fabrics, patterns and shapes were seen by Kansas Citians as well as those who came by train to participate in the activities.

Chapter 3

Petticoat Lane

Because I believe that the next twenty-five years in Kansas City are going to be as great and even greater than the last twenty-five have been; because I expect that these next twenty-five years will see a growth even more sensational and astonishing in this part of the country than I myself observed in my own commercial experience here, I felt justified in building up to the future.

—Siegmund Harzfeld[18]

S even years after the redesign of the Main Street location, construction began on a new ten-story building that would be leased by the store at the southeast corner of Petticoat Lane and Main Street. This is the original location where Lewis Deardorff started his lumberyard after the Civil War. His son, Frank, moved the lumber business to Eighteenth Street and Holmes and built a four-story structure for retail and office space in 1885. A fire destroyed the building in January 1892. The next building, now being razed to make way for the new Parisian, was occupied by Browning, King & Company, a haberdashery for men and boys that was relocated east to Eleventh and Grand.[19]

The new building was designed by Kansas City architect John W. McKecknie (1862–1934). The exterior was faced with ornamental tile, which was made of terra cotta and glazed in a cream color. To support the local economy, when possible, materials that could be bought in Kansas City were used. The formal opening took place on November 30, 1913. Employees worked until midnight the night before, moving merchandise

Detail from a photo of the Waldheim Building (left), showing the construction of the steel framework of the Deardorff Building (right), which was leased to Harzfeld's at the southeast corner of Eleventh Street (Petticoat Lane) and Main Street in 1913. *Missouri Valley Special Collections, Kansas City Public Library, Kansas City, MO. Anderson Photo Company.*

Siegmund Harzfeld, *'Mongst Us* 6, no. 1, March 1929. *Collection of Beth Robinson.*

across the street to its new home. Display windows were backed with intricately grained, rich brown Circassian walnut. The walls were painted in soft yellows, with rugs and window treatments in soft shades of brown. Many of the interior fixtures were of Circassian walnut.[20]

The opening provided Mr. Harzfeld an opportunity to express his dreams for the store's future and the role the building could play in making them happen:

We have built up to the limit of modern capacity, we believe, for the comfort of the shoppers of Kansas City and the surrounding country…We will be as ready to meet the demands of Kansas City today, with the finest and best equipped specialty store the present building world could make for us.

One ambition has always been before my mind since the days when the idea of opening the first specialty store in the Southwest brought me to locate in Kansas City and establish The Parisian Cloak Company. To accomplish this ambition, I have spent the last twenty-three years in studying the problems of women's merchandising, not only in America, but in Europe. The problems are essentially problems of service. And it is only in such a building as our present new home, with such equipment, that it would be possible to hope for anything like the accomplishment of the ambition of which I speak.[21]

As the store approached its twenty-fifth year, Sieg suffered the loss of his mother, Caroline, at the age of seventy. In her honor, the store closed for a day after her passing on January 12, 1914. In June, a new beauty salon opened on the tenth floor, with a separate area for children.[22] In November, the one-year-old building was decorated with silver inside and out to celebrate the quarter-century anniversary of the business.

Ragtime music was all the rage in 1914, when Euday L. Bowman (1887–1949) wrote a famous rag named after the street to the south of Harzfeld's. With the success of the "Twelfth Street Rag," Bowman followed up with songs named for other Kansas City streets, including Harzfeld's address,

Harzfeld's location on Petticoat Lane, circa 1946.

represented by both "Eleventh Street Rag" and "Petticoat Lane Rag." None of the later songs matched the success of the "Twelfth Street Rag," of which the published sheet music sold well for the J.W. Jenkins' Sons Music Company of Kansas City.

In 1948, a proposal introduced by the Public Works Department suggested that the beloved shopping district undergo a narrowing of the

Postcards with views looking east down Petticoat Lane from Main Street. As buildings grew taller, the cards changed from horizontal to vertical.

Illustration of Petticoat Lane looking east from Main Street with Harzfeld's on the right.

street to better accommodate the throngs of shoppers on the sidewalks. A count taken on September 22 showed that between the hours of 11:00 a.m. and 6:00 p.m., 38,933 pedestrians used the walkways. The peak period for the north sidewalk was 5,000 persons per hour, and 3,000 per hour on the south. Some shoppers were forced into the street because of crowding, but the narrowing solution meant that the merchants surrendered on-street parking, which was unpopular. The plans were shelved, and the sidewalks remained bustling.[23]

The famous scene of Petticoat Lane viewed from the west was recreated in an illustration and reproduced on packaging, scarves, handkerchiefs and more. It was a popular subject matter for postcards and became identified with Kansas City. Many people believe that the name given to Eleventh Street between Grand Avenue and Main Street comes from the gusts of wind that would swirl around the streets and expose ladies' petticoats. More likely, it was passed down from the historic fashion and clothing market of the same name on the east end of London, England.

Chapter 4

Stars and Stripes

World War I had begun in Europe, and by the end of 1917, the United States was brought into the conflict. Harzfeld's encouraged the women of the store to register with the Red Cross Women's Committee and provided a registration booth in the store. The committee coordinated war efforts by women and recognized their contributions. This empowerment helped advance women's right to vote in 1920. The war lessened the formalities of fashions of the Victorian age and hemlines rose from the floor to mid-calf length.

Lester Siegel, son of the man who provided the original financing for the Parisian, was in New York, climbing the lower rungs of the merchandising ladder at Bonwit Teller. He was always even-tempered, even when working with temperamental buyers. He came to Kansas City after finding that he had been turned down for officers' training camp due to poor eyesight. He met with Siegmund and discussed opportunities at Harzfeld's, but he still wished to contribute to the war effort. He enlisted in the navy, where he was able to take code messages at the rate of thirty words a minute.[24]

After the war, he chose to return to Kansas City and found himself traveling to markets and learning the ways of the specialty store business as a skirt buyer. He learned quickly, and by 1922, when he married Frieda Levy, he was the vice-president of Harzfeld's.

Lester was born several years after his father financed the store in Kansas City. He grew up in Chicago, in a gray stone house on Michigan Avenue. He graduated from Cornell, where he trained in merchandising

Lester Siegel Sr. (1893–1971), circa 1920s.

and management methods. With his father's connections to his investments in the industry throughout the country, Lester chose to focus his efforts in Kansas City.[25]

The store continued to grow and became a family for many of the employees. A company newsletter organized by Harzfeld's credit union, *'Mongst Us,* named by Sylvia King of the millinery department, was started in 1921.[26]

It is often said that film star Joan Crawford (1905–1977) worked as an elevator operator at Harzfeld's. It is documented that Lucille Fay LeSueur (her birth name, but she also went by Billie Cassin) worked at Kline's in the summer of 1922 and at Emery Bird Thayer in early 1923. It's quite possible, but unclear, that she also had a brief career at Harzfeld's, which was essentially located between the other two stores. When Joan's star rose in Hollywood, she was extremely fashion conscious and an icon of the tailored look of the forties.

In 1923, Harzfeld's opened a small second location in Lawrence, Kansas. Located "On the Hill" at Twelfth and Indiana, it was convenient for students at the University of Kansas.[27] The younger customer was emblematic of the focus of fashion, and hemlines rose just below the knee. This location opened the same year of the first Kansas Relays in the newly completed Memorial Stadium.

A third location opened on Friday, March 8, 1929, on Ninth Street in downtown Columbia, Missouri.[28] Ninth Street soon adopted the label "Petticoat Lane," following in the footsteps of Kansas City. This location also served a college crowd with Stephens College, Columbia College and the University of Missouri nearby. Sieg and other employees would boast about how fast they could travel between the Columbia store and Kansas City.

In 1922, the Petticoat Lane store expanded up and added an eleventh floor, which would house an employee cafeteria. The new addition was inset slightly and was not visible from the street unless a person was at least a half block

Above: Ferdinand and Rose Siegel. These portraits hung on the wall of Lester Siegel Sr.'s office at Harzfeld's.

Below: Glove and hosiery envelope bags, 1928 (dated from an enclosed receipt).

Employee "family tree," illustration by employee Doris Altic. *'Mongst Us* 6, no. 2, April 1929. *Collection of Beth Robinson.*

Left: Newspaper ad, circa 1920s. Newspaper and date unknown.

Below: Columbia store interior. *'Mongst Us* 6, no. 4, June 1929. *Collection of Beth Robinson.*

Ad from the University of Kansas yearbook. The actual street address at this time was listed as 1144 Indiana Street. *Jayhawker*, 1927.

Opposite, top: Harzfeld's "invitations" from Stella Platt, 1925 (top) and 1930 (bottom).

Opposite, bottom: Photo postcard from Columbia, Missouri Harzfeld's, circa 1930s.

away. Three years later, it was extended to the east, leasing the Lillis Building.[29] The roof of the new expansion became a favorite hangout of employees.

As Harzfeld's expanded regionally, locally the Country Club Plaza became America's first major suburban shopping center, opening in 1923.

It became an inspiration and model for retail developments nationally and globally. The area was created by J.C. Nichols for the planned surrounding residential areas and shoppers arriving by automobiles. It featured Spanish-style architecture and became a destination for visitors to Kansas City as well as a future home for another expansion of Harzfeld's.[30]

Over the years, Harzfeld's built an extensive network of buyers for the store. One such buyer, Stella Platt, was featured on numerous direct mail pieces in the '20s. Her "invitations" to the store told of her travels and new items that were awaiting customers. Colorful Victorian fashion illustrations or Louis Icart (1888–1950) artwork graced the covers.

According to Nelly Don historian Terence O'Malley, in 1916, Nell Donnelly started manufacturing housedresses in her living room and later her attic. Harzfeld's was one of several stores in the Kansas City area that initially rejected her designs, but by the time this ad appeared in the *Star*, the Donnelly Garment Company of Kansas City was manufacturing five thousand dresses a day and had become the largest dress manufacturer of the twentieth century. Harzfeld's was one of the many stores across the country to carry Nelly Don dresses.

Harzfeld's ad featuring Nelly Don fashions. In 2006, Terence O'Malley produced both a film and a book, *Nelly Don: A Stitch in Time*, documenting the story of this ground-breaking woman and her Kansas City garment business. *Kansas City Star*, May 4, 1930.

Children's promotional ball and jack set, circa 1930s.

Dressing the children of Kansas City and the region had been a focus of the store since its start. Promotional items, such as the *Juvenile Magazine*, and branded items, such as the jacks in the image above, were innovative ways to reach its young customers. The bag for the jacks promotes fitting of shoes by X-ray method. Fluoroscope machines were in wide use nationally by the 1940s in many stores that sold shoes. The child, guardian and salesperson were able to view the bone structure through portals in the machine. Once it was discovered in the early '50s that the exposure to radiation through the X-rays might be harmful, these machines were removed from stores.

Logos and type treatments for the specialty store played a large part in defining its image. The type treatment for the first print ad in 1891 was likely typeset by one of the local newspapers. The dropping capital "P" and the curling swashes of the display type made for a handsome introduction. There were numerous variations on type treatments in the early years. The upper floors of the Main Street location had an exposed south exterior brick wall that served as a large-scale sign with bold sans serif type (see image on page 18). An early version had script type.

HARZFELD'S

HARZFELD'S PARISIAN
PETTICOAT LANE—KANSAS CITY

Harzfeld's
PETTICOAT LANE

HARZFELD'S

HARZFELD'S

Harzfeld's

Harzfeld's

Harzfeld's

Harzfelds

HARZFELDS

HARZFELDS

The evolution of type treatments and logos for the Parisian Cloak Company and Harzfeld's.

42

A "trademark" introduced in an 1890s ad was composed of type set on an arrow, a recognizable icon, but not a good choice for a logo. With the type reading upright, it pointed to the left, directing the reader away from the advertisement. It was sometimes pointed right with no regard to the type reading upside down.

As Paris was seen as the center of fashion, many stores throughout the country shared similar or even the same name as the Parisian. Adler's Millinery, one block to the south, featured its "Salon Parisian," and the "Paris" millinery shop was directly across the street. This may have led to Sieg putting his own name "on the line." A heraldic-type shield with an "H" was used as an architectural element early in the century. After the move to Petticoat Lane, "Harzfeld's Parisian" and then simply "Harzfeld's" soon stood alone as the store's more distinctive name. The new building also provided an even larger south-facing brick façade to emblazon the Harzfeld's name, this time in bold stacked sans serif type. A bold, outlined logo from the '20s felt as though it was dancing the Charleston. The '30s saw a number of variations, from a streamlined condensed type to a script that optimistically climbed upward to recover from the economics of the time and would have looked right at home rendered in chrome on the back of a sedan.

The '40s moved toward a condensed logo. The verticals of the letter forms continued to be accentuated just prior to losing their legibility. This version of the logo, attributed to display director Erasmus "Ras" Beall, is the one most people remember. It was part of an encompassing identity system, which included the use of green in the logo and distinctive green and white stripes that would adorn everything from packaging and advertisements to decorative elements in the stores. Even green ribbons were installed in the office typewriters to continue the look onto company stationery. This national award-winning identity system was so successful that it was still in use through the 1970s.

The final logo, inspired by the Sakowitz department store's identity system, was introduced in 1980. A descender coming off of the "R" kissed the "Z" to make it unique and anchored at the center point. The new colors were burgundy and gray. Although the letter forms were beautiful, it was not nearly as distinctive, or loved, as the previous iconic identity system.

Harzfeld's created and trademarked a number of exclusive private labels, including Gadabout, for sportswear, shoes and children's wear, and K-50, primarily for suits. Its most successful label was adapted from its famous address, Petticoat Lane. The trademark was applied to dresses, hosiery, shoes and its own fine French perfume. The fragrance

Left: Petticoat Lane French perfume. *Collection of Helen Farnsworth, all rights reserved.*

Below: "The new ultra-modern perfume bar on the first floor. Behind it: Nora Bynan and Madge Sheffler." *Petticoat Laner* 4, no. 1, January 1949.

was available in a simple dram bottle but also in an elegant black glass version. Leveraging Harzfeld's relationship with the designer Hattie Carnegie (1889–1956) of New York, the store was able to borrow the bottle design by Julien Viard for her New Year's Eve fragrance, which was introduced about 1924. It is an exact copy except for the wording on the label and the Harzfeld's crest or heraldic-type shield. The bottle was 2⅞ inches in height. The cap was a gold over black glass-ground stopper, and the bottom of the bottle was embossed with "Made in France." According to Helen Farnsworth, archivist for the International Perfume Bottle Association (IPBA), this presentation was very high style and a good representation of both French Deco and earlier Japanese-style work.

The unusual name of the fragrance became the brunt of a joke in a 1931 issue of the *Chilocothe Constitution-Tribune*: "*Petticoat Lane* perfume is advertised by one of the Kansas City stores; the other Kansas City perfume, *Packing House Avenue* does its own advertising."

The first men's night was held in December 1939. This event was geared toward the male shopper who may have found himself a bit out of his element but needed to find a stylish gift for the lady in his life. The evening offered refreshments on the house and the entertainment of a fashion show, and hosts and hostesses were available "to help you make wise gift selections." The upscale gift directory included the ever popular perfume, jewelry and furs, but also ranged from cruise clothes to negligees and silver to fine crystal. Children's gifts and toys were an added bonus for the one-stop shopping excursion.

On December 7, 1941, America was brought into World War II after an attack by the Japanese in Pearl Harbor. Many male employees left for service. A number of retired ladies came back to fill the positions of the men who left and of women who went to work in factories. Everyone was encouraged to buy defense bonds. Deliveries were pared down as rubber tires were not available. Boxes and paper items were used frugally, and employees were encouraged to do without some items and to save foil from their gum and cigarette wrappers. Defense uniforms were available on the fourth floor. Employees were encouraged to speak of courage rather than of the dangers of the times.[31]

Restrictions on the use of fabric simplified fashion, and efficiency of materials dictated the look. Clever adaptations of suits left behind by men inspired a new look and resulted in fitted suits for women with broad padded shoulders.

Fashion illustration by Norma Butterfield, circa 1940. A similar ad from October 1942 headlined: "'Be Cigarette Slim' in tobacco tones!" A sheer wool crepe dress was shown, available in "tobacco brown" and "bright leaf green." In a separate promotion, Sapphire brand nylon stockings in an "exciting new fashion color," old gold, were also sold in novelty packaging, wrapped to look like Old Gold brand cigarettes.

Interior of Petticoat Lane store, third floor, circa 1940s. *Photo by Harkins Commercial Photo.*

Petticoat Lane Harzfeld's decorated for Christmas, circa 1940s.

Above, left: Siegmund Harzfeld (1868–1944).

Above, right: Florence Harzfeld. *Courtesy of* The Independent, *January 17, 1952.*

A "Victory Bar" was created on the first floor of the store. Customers were encouraged to bring in their laundered hosiery to make powder bags. Furs were to be altered into vests for the Merchant Marines, and items such as compacts were received for their metal. Books and magazines were collected to be redistributed to servicemen. As of April 1942, $13,000 in war bonds had been sold through the Harzfeld's credit union.

With strong connections to its suppliers, the store was able to secure fashions and non-rationed merchandise. As more women entered the workforce, their disposable income enabled Harzfeld's to continue and even prosper during this difficult time.

In February 1944, the Harzfelds celebrated their fiftieth wedding anniversary at the Muehlebach Hotel with an open invitation to their friends. A surprise performance by the Kansas City Symphony lasted late into the evening. Sadly, one month later, on March 6, Sieg passed away at the age of seventy-six. Lester Siegel Sr. assumed the position as president of Harzfeld's.

Six charities benefited from over a half million dollars from the estate of the Harzfelds. One beneficiary, the University of Kansas City (now UMKC), was able to establish its first endowed chair, the Harzfeld Professor

Lester Siegel Sr. illustration by Bill Lacy from the Kansas City Athletic Club, *Blue Diamond* (cartoon edition), December 1930.

of Economics and Business Policy. Lester Siegel Sr. assisted Florence in realizing these gifts in a way that enabled her to witness the funds benefit the causes that the Harzfelds held dear before her passing. Florence passed away in 1952 at the age of eighty-two.

In 1946, a comprehensive list of star designers and labels was compiled for a fifty-fifth-anniversary publication.[32]

Aberle	Billy Gordon	Chester Barrie
Adrian	Bloch Freres	Ciro
Alice May	Braemar	Claire McCardell
Andrew Geller	British Walkers	Clarepotter
Ann Haviland	Bryan	Cobblers
Anthony Blotta	Cangemi	Coty
Barbizon	Carlin	Davidow
Ben Reig	Carmel	Dawnelle
B.H. Wragge	Charbert	De De Johnson

Fifty-fifth-anniversary cover of *Petticoat Laner* 1, no. 3, February 1946.

Darrell Porter cartoon of Lester Siegel Sr.'s tenth-floor office, from a fifty-fifth-anniversary commemorative booklet.

De Liso Debs	Fredrica	Jerro
Delman	Gadabout	Joan Frazier
Diana	Germaine Monteil	Johara
Dix-Make	Gershel	John Frederics
Dorian	Glen Bogie	Josef
Dorothy Hubbs	Glenhunt	Joyce
Dorothy O'Hara	Gold Stripe	Juliette
Dorothy Thorpe	Gotham	Junior Firsts
D'orsay	Greencrest	K-50
Edith Lances	Habitmakers	Kay Dunhill
Edna Vilm	Handmacher	Kay Fuchs
Elizabeth Arden	Hartnell	Kaylon
Emily Wilkins	Hattie Carnegie	Kislav
Esther Dorothy	Herb Farm	Korell
Faberge	Hobe	Koret
Florence Gainor	Isabel	Kraus
Frances Denney	Jablow	Larkwood
Francette	Jaccard	La Tausca
Frederick Lunning	Jantzen	Lavando

Lesterfield
Lewis
Lilly Dache
Louella Ballerino
Louise Barnes
  Gallagher
Margie Joy
Maria Rass
Marie Earle
Mark Cross
Mary Chess
Maurice Rentner
Mazer
Meramby
Midtown
Mme. Adrienne
Morris Wolock
Napier
Natacha Brooks
Natalie Nicoli
Nathan Krauskopf
Nettie Rosenstein
Northridge
North Star
Palter De Liso
Patou
Patullo
Paula Brooks
Petti, Jr.
Petticoat Lane
Phelps
Poirette
Princess Pat
Propper
Radelle
Rosenblum
Sapphire
Schiaparelli
Seymour Troy

Shirley
Spalding
Sportsters
Surrey
Susan Wayne
Suzanne Augustine
Tabu
Tigere
Tina Leser
Trifari
Tru-Balance
Urbanites
Vanity Fair
Vanta
Vassar
Voris
Winfield

Chapter 5

The Mural

In the fall of 1946, Lester Siegel Sr. commissioned famed Kansas City artist Thomas Hart Benton to create a mural for the Petticoat Lane store. Lester and Tom met at the store one evening to review the horizontal space above the elevators for which the mural was to be created. Tom lit a pipe and surveyed the location, taking into account the distance, vantage point and scale of the project. Despite Tom's controversial subjects of the past, he was given freedom in choosing the subject matter, but Lester asked him "try to let me stay in business."[33] Tom suggested the retelling of the mythological story of Achelous and Hercules applied to a Midwestern setting. It would portray the struggle for the favor of a Greek princess between Hercules and the river god, Achelous, who has assumed the shape of a bull and is symbolic of man's struggle with the Missouri River and conquest of its broad and fertile valley.[34]

The entire process of the mural was documented in an eleven-minute color film. Encylopædia Britannica Films contracted with the Calvin Company of Kansas City to produce the documentary, called *The Making of a Mural*. The local company produced industrial films in 16mm format and, during World War II, created training and safety films. Benton's process, from the initial sketches through the final installation, was recorded to be retold to numerous groups and schools. Included below is a recounting from the film in part.

In his studio at 3616 Belleview, Tom began with abstract sketches, creating rhythms across a horizontal plane. Following these rhythms, Benton drew a new pencil sketch with discernible forms in the scene, but still with few

Achelous and Hercules, 1947, by Thomas Hart Benton (1889–1975). Tempera on canvas, 62⁷/₈ x 264¹/₈. *Gift of Allied Stores Corporation, and museum purchase through the Smithsonian Institution Collections Acquisition Program. Smithsonian American Art Museum, Washington, D.C. Art © Benton Testamentary Trusts/UMB Bank Trustee/Licensed by VAGA, New York, NY.*

detailed elements. He then sculpted a clay model of the forms, a technique that he used in much of his work to envision the appropriate depth, light and shadow. Next, he created three small-scale, detailed color paintings as options to be discussed with Lester in moving forward.[35]

Live models were then brought in for Benton to construct more detail. Mr. Siegel's daughter, Marjorie, served as the muse for the Greek princess Dejanira, just to the right of Hercules, who was modeled by her husband, William Navran, in the center of the painting. Benton sketched the models and also sculpted greater detailed clay figures.

He then created an outline drawing or "cartoon." The process took on a more mechanical phase as the elements were divided into a grid, which served as a guide to scale up and transfer the image to the large canvas. The canvas, at over five feet tall and twenty-two feet wide, was divided into the same grid work, and the square by square transferring of elements began.

Lines gave way to paint as Benton applied a tempera made from egg yolks and pigment. He would continually step back to look at the work through a diminishing glass. This allowed him to assess the color and see what the painting would look like from a distance. After the foreground elements were completed, Benton went back and painted in the sky. He mixed seven different blues and added Vinylite and beeswax to the paint to allow for smooth, gradual blending.

After applying layers of wax, the painting was complete. The unwieldy canvas was carefully removed from the studio space to make its trip downtown, just over three miles away. The entire process for this mural took nearly eight months.

Harzfeld's reproduced the artwork on postcards and advertisements. Promotions were created based on the mural, with fashions in "Benton

Clockwise, from top left:
Marjorie Navran, daughter of
Lester Siegel Sr., posed for the
woman to the right of Hercules,
who was modeled by her husband,
William.

Vice-president since 1946, Maurice
Breyer, a friend of Thomas Hart
Benton, in his office with Benton
lithograph, *Instruction*, 1940. Breyer
started as secretary of Harzfeld's
in 1939 with expertise in millinery
and merchandising.

Petticoat Lane location, interior
of main level with mural installed
above elevators.

Petticoat Lane location, interior
of main level, north wall. *Patricia
DuBose Duncan Collection, Kansas
Collection, RH MS 535, Kenneth
Spencer Research Libraries, University of
Kansas, 1979.*

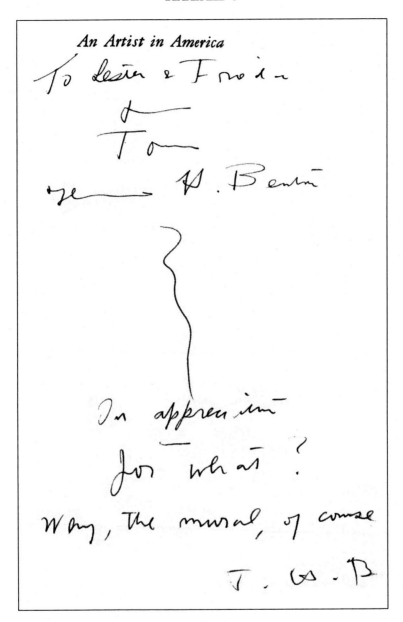

Inscription by Thomas Hart Benton to Lester and Frieda Siegel on the inside of his book, *An Artist in America.*

Originally a carriage house and stable, Thomas Hart Benton's studio is just south of his home at 3616 Belleview, Kansas City, Missouri. The studio and home are now a state historic site and available for tours.

Benton chats with model Lucille Renfro. Dorothy Hall stands behind at a Chamber of Commerce Fashion Show. *Petticoat Laner*, February 1950.

brown" and "straw hat yellow." The store provided visitors with a small folding flyer of Benton's telling of the Greek myth. The mural was included in an updated version of Benton's biography, *An Artist in America*.

In 1956, as part of a redesign of the store's main floor, the mural was moved across the room, to the north wall opposite the elevators.

"He could see the connection between fine art and fashion: he came up with the idea that we should have a fine piece of art in our store for customers to enjoy." Lester's son, Lester Siegel Jr., has also commented that it was Harzfeld's finest possession and one of its best investments.[36]

Chapter 6

Displaying Fashion Forward

Our relations with Paris have been so developed, such close connections have been formed for this new specialty store of ours with the great style authorities who dictate the policies of dress for women the world over, that we are guaranteed as is perhaps no other specialty store on this side of the water, the receiving of correct and authoritative style information, the moment it appears.
—Siegmund Harzfeld, 1913[37]

Harzfeld's was the largest women's specialty store in Kansas City, one of the largest in the Midwest, and was known for its high quality of merchandise, exclusivity and personalized attention and service. It had a national reputation and acceptance, partly due to the placements of advertising in fashion and fashion-aware magazines, including *Bride's Magazine, Charm, Glamour, Harper's Bazaar, Harper's Junior Bazaar, House & Garden, House Beautiful, Mademoiselle, Seventeen, Town & Country* and *Vogue.* For magazine ads where a couture fashion was featured, it was often the practice/agreement that the store would purchase two of the garments. Usually chosen were a petite size and a larger size that could more easily be altered.

The trend-setting specialty store was known as a mecca for the elegant and fashion-conscious woman. Harzfeld's image had been built on affording its patrons with a comprehensive collection of leading world designers. Couture labels in the French Room included Norman Norell and Christian Dior and, later, Halston, Bill Blass and others. Another high fashion department, the Shoe Salon, carried a variety of famous labels.

View from Macy's looking east down Petticoat Lane. In 1947, Macy's acquired John Taylor's, which was started as a dry goods store in 1881. The name change took place after a remodeling and expansion of the building in 1949.

The distinctive store carried affordable women's and children's apparel and accessories at moderate prices. Every effort was made to ensure that the customer on a limited budget was offered fashion-right selections of merchandise in most attractive surroundings.

While maintaining valuable relationships on the East Coast, Lester Sr. found that there were also new designers on the West Coast whose fashions appealed to the women of Kansas City. Many of these designers, such as Adrian, Irene and Howard Greer, worked as costume designers for the Hollywood stars. This sometimes allowed for exciting cross promotions with local movie houses. Costume designer Edith Head's sketches for Betty Hutton's wardrobe in *Incendiary Blonde* were displayed in the windows in 1945.[38] Eight windows, two displaying movie projectors, were devoted to the Oscar award–winning *Best Years of Our Lives* in 1947.[39]

One of the store's biggest cross promotions came in 1960 for *Midnight Lace*, starring Doris Day. An early private premiere of the film and a six-minute featurette promoting the fashions by Irene was shown to the sales staff. This

Harzfeld's

Blenko Glass

Decorative as well as useful. Grand for shower, wedding and hostess gifts. Sketched from a collection!

Pitcher, crackle with green handle, **1.95**
Double Lipped Pitcher, ruby color, **2.25**
Also comes blue, green, crystal at **1.75**
Ruby Color Tumblers, generous size, **1.75**

Gift Shop . . . 8th

Harzfeld's advertisement featuring Blenko Glass from Milton, West Virginia. Blenko diversified from sheet glass into vases during the Depression, and by the end of World War II it had expanded its line of items and ramped up production to meet consumer demand. Fashionable, branded items such as Russel Wright dinnerware and Jensen silver were also popular gift items. Numerous unbranded gift and decorative items were also offered to customers. *Courtesy of* The Independent, *May 22, 1948.*

Adrian ad prepared by Carl Reimers Co., Inc., New York. *Town & Country*, March 1952.

Opposite, top: Designer Howard Greer with model at Harzfeld's showing, 1950.

Opposite, bottom: Runway in third-floor French Room during Howard Greer showing, 1950.

Left: Irene gown at Harzfeld's fashion show, 1949.

Below: *Harper's Bazaar* window display with surrealist hand by Erasmus Beall, circa 1940.

allowed for an informed promotion, which included a contest with a grand prize of an original suit by Irene, as seen in the film.[40]

Promotional opportunities with movie houses, live theatre and musical performances continued to be main stage in window designs. The windows promoted the latest fashions, but they also performed the purpose of enticement and an invitation to participate in some manner in the goings-on of the day, reflecting society, culture and art.

Erasmus Beall was Harzfeld's display director for thirty-three years. He was a shy southern gentleman of great creative talent, born in Dawson, Georgia. He found his first display opportunities at Rich's in Atlanta, where he was remembered for a bridal window with rice scattered outside on the sidewalk.[41] He started with the store as early as 1936. He introduced the familiar green and white stripe graphic treatment with the condensed logo about 1940. He left to serve in the war, where he was with a camouflage unit of combat engineers and received the Purple Heart and three battle stars.

At different times, he taught classes at the Kansas City Art Institute, created window displays for Cricket West and appears to have designed a logo with a coordinating zebra pattern for Chasnoff's. While in New York, he created campaigns for Revlon, was invited to judge art displays at the 1939 World's Fair and designed for events at the Waldorf Astoria. When Kansas City celebrated its centennial in 1950, Ras created the set designs for Big Birthday, an elaborate, highly scripted fashion show sponsored by the garment manufacturers. He also opened a decorative accessories shop at 4222 Main called Et Cetera, not far from the Wishbone Restaurant, originator of the now famous salad dressing. He lived above that eatery for a time. He was said to sometimes have a hint of garlic on him.

Beall returned to Harzfeld's in the early '50s. His office was in the basement, a treasure-trove of wild and wonderful things. His wife, Aileen, also worked in the display department. He suggested themed, animated Christmas window displays for the Petticoat Lane store in 1952. The windows, featuring dancing Dresden dolls, snowmen and elaborate settings, were a sensation! Thousands lined the streets to see the displays. Mr. Siegel introduced a Distinguished Merit Award to recognize Ras for the achievement, and the engaging Christmas windows became a holiday tradition, delighting children and adults alike for many years to come.[42]

Harzfeld's celebrated several milestone anniversaries. Its sixtieth was in 1951. Beall, along with Thelma Kennedy, head of advertising, came up with the concept "We love Petticoat Lane" and the idea of wearing our "Heart

Erasmus Beall's display department staff, 1950. *Front, left to right:* "Mike," Lloyd Hyatt, "Dell," Jerry Correa, "Joe." *Rear, left to right:* Clifford "Mac" McWaid, "John."

Opposite, top: Harzfeld's display window, circa 1940s, promoting a lecture series at the Nelson Art Gallery and Atkins Museum of Fine Art in February to benefit Chinese War Orphans. *Photo by Anderson K.C. Saddle Horse, eighth century CE. Tang Dynasty (618–906 CE.). Earthenware with three-color lead glaze. Height: 27" (68.6 cm). Gift of Mr. Sadajiro Yamanaka, 32-67. The Nelson-Atkins Museum of Art.*

Opposite, bottom: Harzfeld's display window, circa 1940s. *Photo by Anderson K.C. Objects from the Nelson-Atkins Museum of Art.*

Christmas display window of a winter scene. From the cover of a late 1970s Harzfeld's Christmas catalogue.

Christmas display window with grandmother looking on as a girl with feather tickles the nose of a sleeping boy in lower bunk. From the cover of a late 1970s Harzfeld's Christmas catalogue.

Above: Brush calligraphy alphabet by Erasmus Beall, circa 1950. *Collection of Clifton (Mac) McWaid.*

Left: Christmas display window featuring ice skaters from the *Petticoat Laner*, December 1953.

Lester Siegel Sr. presenting Erasmus Beall with the first Distinguished Merit Award in 1952.

on Our Sleeve." They convinced West and East Coast designers to create "sleeves" to be displayed in the windows along with their fashions. It was a successful promotion with many designers participating, including Adrian, Irene, Howard Greer and William Cahill on the West Coast, and Nettie Rosenstein, Hattie Carnegie, Anthony Blotta and Davidow among the East Coast designers. It received great press in the papers when the "sleeves" arrived on a flight via Trans World Airlines, Inc., which was headquartered in Kansas City. TWA was often flown by Harzfeld's buyers, and many collaborations with the airlines took place over the years.

A similar promotion was created for the sixty-fifth anniversary in '56, this time with "leaves" and the theme "Eve's Leaves." Designers from both coasts again submitted their unique creations. Irene made a special appearance at the store during the promotion. Female employees wore leaf corsages with ribbons and jewels; men wore small gold leaves on their lapels. Packaging was enhanced with gold labels featuring a sketch of "Eve," the first fashion-conscious woman sporting the first fashion: the leaf.[43]

Late in his life, Ras Beall worked in security at the Nelson-Atkins Museum of Art. Marc Wilson, museum director of twenty-eight years, comments on Ras and his talents: "He was the foremost interior decorator and window designer of his day...he was in the artsy world of Kansas City, a person of great standing."

Chapter 7

Everything's Up to Date

Harzfeld's was ready to expand and remodel to meet the needs of its postwar customers. There were many restrictions on performing upgrades and remodeling to stores during the war. Although air conditioning had been installed in some stores before the war, the systems needed upgrading. New business machines and new sizes of fluorescent lighting became available, and new materials had been developed for flooring and fixtures. The needs of the consumer and traffic flow were scientifically analyzed and this was applied to the layout and function of existing and new stores. "Visual merchandising" replaced terms such as display and decorating. There was demand for jobs in the developing suburban areas, and Harzfeld's started expanding to meet the need.

The first remodeling came to the exterior of the store on Petticoat Lane. Travertine marble was installed from the top of the show windows to the bottom of the second-story windows. Earlier alterations had already deviated from the original design. The display windows became recessed and lined with antique verde marble. Large wooden "frames" were removed from the perimeter of the windows, and the backgrounds were replaced with stained red birch.

Another early modernization effort came to the Columbia location in 1949, when it moved from 20 South Ninth Street to 922 East Broadway. The new store reflected all the aspirations of America in the postwar era: a well thought out space, bright lighting, large windows and a streamlined façade. It must have been a welcome change for Leo and Lois Van Coutren, who had managed the store since 1938.

Before and after proposed modifications to the overall façade and photos of entrance on Main, circa 1949.

Clifford "Mac" McWaid enjoyed entertaining the college girls while he decorated the display window in the evenings, circa 1950. The window was usually redone each week. Mac started at the Petticoat Lane store in Kansas City. When he moved to Columbia, his display work helped pay his way through school.

Harzfeld's Columbia store interior, circa 1950.

Country Club Plaza Harzfeld's location. *Photograph by Richard Garfinkel.*

The largest expansion took place in 1954 with the addition of the three-level Country Club Plaza store on the southeast corner of Nichols Road and Pennsylvania Avenue. The store was designed by Neville, Sharp and Simon architects and Edward W. Tanner and Associates, AIA. This was an entirely new structure, designed from the ground up. Just as the design of this shopping area had taken into account the customer arriving by automobile some forty years earlier, the new store integrated parking into the design. Three hundred cars could "park on the roof" in an attached parking structure and enter on the upper level. The store covered fifty-five thousand square feet. The adobe brick exterior was painted a soft gray-green, with windows lined in antique verde marble.

A focal point of the store was a large, open, spiral staircase. The store was lit in part with sophisticated brass lighting fixtures by Finnish designer Paavo Tynell. The window treatments were hand-woven with hemp, suede, metal and wooden beads by Miria Kipp of California.[44] The rubber tile floor was in shades of rich brown, black and café au lait. Green and white stripes adorned the inside of the elevators. Over twenty-nine thousand

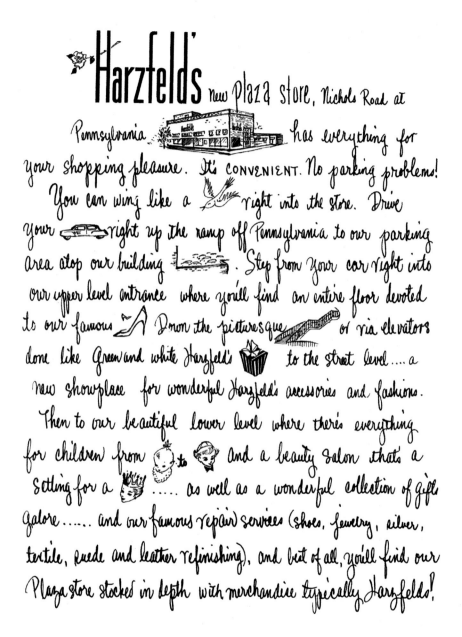

Harzfelds new Plaza store, Nichols Road at Pennsylvania has everything for your shopping pleasure. It's CONVENIENT. No parking problems! You can wing like a [bird] right into the store. Drive your [car] right up the ramp off Pennsylvania to our parking area atop our building [parking]. Step from your car right into our upper level entrance where you'll find an entire floor devoted to our famous [shoe]. Down the picturesque [stairs] or via elevators done like Green and white Harzfeld's [gift box] to the street level..... a new showplace for wonderful Harzfeld's accessories and fashions. Then to our beautiful lower level where there's everything for children from [baby] to [girl] and a beauty salon that's a setting for a [face] ..... as well as a wonderful collection of gifts galore...... and our famous repair services (shoes, jewelry, silver, textile, suede and leather refinishing), and best of all, you'll find our Plaza store stocked in depth with merchandise typically Harzfelds!

Announcement with pictograms welcoming customers to the new Plaza store in 1954.

79

Country Club Plaza Harzfeld's. A dramatic spiraling stairway lit by a Tynell lighting fixture, circa 1954.

Opposite, top: Country Club Plaza Harzfeld's. Elevator with green and white stripe interior, circa 1954. It has been said that recordings by Marilyn Monroe were played to announce the floors you were arriving on.

Opposite, bottom: Country Club Plaza Harzfeld's. Children's area featuring cat-shaped bird cage with live canary, circa 1954.

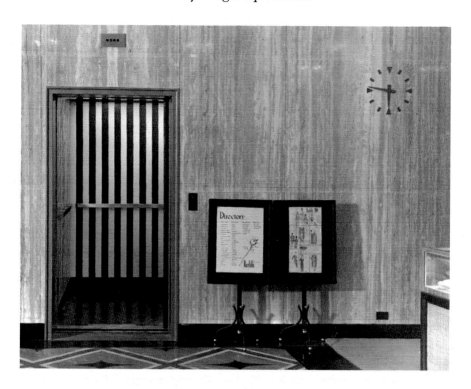

Top: Interior of Lawrence, Kansas location, circa 1950.

Bottom: Lawrence, Kansas location at Twelfth and Indiana with the Band Box Beauty Salon around the right side, circa 1950.

Blue Ridge Harzfeld's, 1958.

pounds of steel were used in the construction of custom-built shelves for shoe stock. All the furnishings were custom made exclusively for the store. Eighteenth-century terra cotta statues from France graced the ready-to-wear section. Aileen Beall of the display department created smart black-and-white drawings for the powder rooms. The new store was staffed by 160 personnel.[45]

A casual opening occurred on April 4 to avoid the crush that follows a public announcement. Small cards attached to the entrance doors simply read "Open today."

Lorene Roberson, associate and Metcalf South store manager, remembers that Joy perfume by Jean Patou, a flowery fragrance with a blend of oils including jasmine and rose, was filtered through the ventilation system. Lorie Newhouse, a merchandise manager and later vice-president, brought this and many other fine fragrances to Kansas City.[46]

The new Plaza store kept good fashion company with stores like Swanson's, Peck & Peck, Chasnoff's, Rothschild's, Emery Bird Thayer, Mindlin's and Cricket West. There were also Sears, Wolferman's and Helzberg's Jewelry.

Focus turned back to the Petticoat Lane location in 1956 when the first floor had its ceiling lowered and covered with acoustical tile. The lighting was also upgraded. The Thomas Hart Benton mural was moved to the

Above: Blue Ridge Mall Harzfeld's, millinery, 1958. Décor likely the work of Jack Rees. *Photograph by Randazzo and Morrison.*

Below: Blue Ridge Mall Harzfeld's, 1958. Décor likely the work of Jack Rees. *Photograph by Randazzo and Morrison.*

north wall, opposite the elevators, which were refaced with pink Norwegian marble. New counters and cases were put in, and a more efficient air-conditioning system was also installed. Many other renovations continued throughout the building.[47]

Although upgrades had been made to the Lawrence location, the store was closed in the mid-'50s. It is more recently remembered as a former site of a Yellow Sub sandwich shop, frequented by students at the University of Kansas to its south. The structure was recently razed to make way for a new seven-story, ninety-two-room hotel, the Oread Inn, opening in 2010.

The Blue Ridge Mall was built just off I-70, where it met up with Highway 40 in eastern Kansas City. It was originally created as an open-air mall in 1958, with Harzfeld's forty-one-thousand-square-foot, two-level space opening November 6. The entrances were flanked with stripes of alternating green, antique verde quarried from Vermont and white marble that was supplied and installed by the Carthage Marble Company of Kansas City.

Chapter 8

The Right Appearance

Patricia "Pat" George studied fashion at the Kansas City Art Institute (KCAI). She attended at the same time as Robert "Bob" Rauschenberg. Both artists were selected to create fashions for the annual Spring Flower Festival at Municipal Auditorium in February 1948. Patricia's dress was of brown linen with organdy poplin, resembling the cup of a jonquil. Rauschenberg designed two dresses. The first, with a coral shantung cape, resembled an inverted corolla of an anthurium blossom. His other dress featured green and white stripes, a fashionable motif, with hoop supports on the outside resembling a trellis with ivy entwined.[48] After he went on to design windows for Bonwit Teller and Tiffany's in New York, he later became one of the foremost American artists of the twentieth century.

Patricia continued to bridge the worlds of fashion and art. Some time after graduating from KCAI in '48, she began working for Harzfeld's in the advertising department. One of her mentors in the department was fashion illustrator Ranald "Ranny" Miller. Patricia was able to capture the essence of fashion and brought a strong conceptual direction and playfulness into her advertisements. She also worked alongside fellow fashion illustrators Mary Catherine (Place) Miller and Alice (Iwanaga) McOsker.

Patricia pursued fine arts, studying with a group of contemporaries under the lead of Frederic James (1915–1985), an American painter who specialized in watercolors, taught at the Art Institute and studied under Benton. Pat traveled with the group around Kansas City, the Flint Hills and beyond capturing landscapes with exquisitely rendered architectural and natural elements.

Ranald Miller illustration, with Patricia George, fellow fashion illustrator, as model, circa early 1950s. *Courtesy of Patricia George.*

Pat spent two decades designing characteristically stylish ads and materials for the firm. Harzfeld's advertised extensively in the *Kansas City Star* and *Kansas City Times.* Tear sheets were reproductions of the ads sent back to the store as proof or verification that the ad had run. These sheets circulated through President Lester Siegel's office. If an ad especially appealed to Mr. Siegel, he would acknowledge this with an encouraging note signed "LS." Lester admired Patricia's work and would often ask her to create playful holiday cards for his personal use. He would also ask her to sketch ideas for jewelry, from which unique pieces were made and given to his wife.

When commenting on her time at Harzfeld's, Patricia said, "It was a wonderful time—I kid you not!"

In November 1958, five of Harzfeld's neighboring stores—Emery Bird Thayer, Jones, Peck's, Kline's and Macy's—were boycotted and picketed by the black community of Kansas City.[49] Each of these stores had segregated cafeterias, while Harzfeld's did not have a public cafeteria. This boycott followed the success of the first sit-in a few months prior in Oklahoma City against Kansas City–based Katz Drug Stores. The stores refused to concede until the spring of 1959.

The 1964 civil rights movement assisted in breaking down acts of discrimination. This helped allow people of all races to be treated equally in employment and commerce. There were many black

Original cover illustration by Ranald Miller of town suit by Adrian. The Independent, *June 21, 1952.*

Patricia George sketches fellow fashion illustrator Mary Catherine (Place) Miller (upper left), who created the artwork in the advertisement to the right in the fall of 1950. Mary later married Frank Miller, an illustrator and Pulitzer Prize–awarded editorial cartoonist for the *Des Moines Register*. Alice (Iwanaga) McOsker (lower left) created the artwork for a 1956 Christmas catalogue (lower right).

This Christian Dior illustration by Patricia George was created for an ad that ran in the *Kansas City Star* on Sunday, January 20, 1957, in honor of the French designer's tenth anniversary of the introduction of what became labeled as the "New Look." A curvaceous silhouette created from a cinched waist and full skirt created from generous amounts of fabric was met with strong reactions after the rationing of fabric during World War II. The ad copy read, "The man whose merest move has for ten years set the fashion world spinning with excitement. The man who, comparatively unknown until 1947, became a sensation overnight. Today that man is still the most famous figure in international fashion...and more than any other single influence in the fashion world. Proudly we salute Christian Dior and his entire staff on celebrating their tenth year. Exclusively the French room, 3rd floor." On October 24, 1957, the designer passed away at age fifty-two. Yves Saint Laurent, his first and only assistant, was named to provide artistic direction for the brand.

Original fashion illustration by Patricia George of "Street-of-Paris" print on silk sheath by Irene. Additional details of the print were realized on the final cover of *The Independent*, December 14, 1957.

employees at Harzfeld's dating back to its early years; most held more service-focused jobs. There were many friendships and examples of respect shown between whites and blacks; however, it's difficult to assess the levels of discrimination that were part of American culture at that time. Improvements surely occurred at all places of business after the civil rights movement took hold. Today, we still have struggles in our stores to ensure equal treatment for all.

The dress purchased at Harzfeld's by Irene Allis to be worn at the January 19, 1961 presidential inauguration eve gala of John F. Kennedy was created by West Coast designer Helga Oppenheimer. It is now part of the collection of the Kansas City Museum, where it is one of the favorite dresses of Lisa Shockley, curatorial specialist. Lisa shares, "The dress is very typical of Helga designs. She was known for close and/or tailor-fitted designs in bold colors. Her evening gowns were known for being both tight and flowing at the same time, and that is very evident from this dress. There are a number of reasons why I love this dress so much. It uses two bold and unusual shades of yellow and green that would look good on only a very few people."

A blizzard hit Washington, D.C., the evening of the gala. Traffic was at a standstill, with cars stalled along the streets. Potential attendees at the Mayflower Hotel had very little luck hailing cabs. Barney Allis stopped a milk truck, offered the driver twenty-five dollars and they were on their way. The Allises invited at least six others to stand in the back of the truck for the trip. They arrived at the National Armory, to the dismay of police security and other guests, without a wrinkle to Irene's beautiful dress. Although the event started late, with only half the invited guests, it was a wonderful evening. Frank Sinatra was a featured performer, along with others, including Gene Kelly, Nat King Cole, Ethel Merman, Bette Davis and Leonard Bernstein.[50] Irene also wore the dress to the 1962 Jewel Ball in Kansas City.

Left: Andy Warhol would have envied this work. Illustration by Patricia George for Sandler of Boston, *Charm*, September 1958.

Below: *Kansas City Star* advertisement, illustration by Patricia George. The copy read, "60 Mercury, For the Well-Planned Getaway; Adele Simpson and Mercury 1960...to arrive in style! Vogue says: 'Travel clothes—to go a long way in fashion.' Here, from the November 1st issue, these Adele Simpson exclusives to follow the sun. Far left: two-tone silk linen sheath. 89.95. Left: silk crepe with crystal pleat hip yoke. 125.00 Right: off-shoulder satin bodice on silk chiffon. 245.00. Far right: silk linen print has a velvet bow. 125.00. French Room, 3rd floor Downtown and Plaza."

Evening gown by Helga, 1960/61. Snapshot of Irene Allis in this dress taken by her husband, Barney, on the balcony of their penthouse at the Muehlebach Hotel. *Courtesy of Union Station/Kansas City Museum.*

GAY GIBSON

15.95

15.95

Original illustration by Patricia George featuring Gay Gibson, a label of the Gernes Garment Company of Kansas City, circa 1960s. The manufacturer had two thousand employees by this time.

Original illustration by Patricia George for advertisement featuring the Kansas City skyline and Revlon, appearing in the *Kansas City Star*, November 19, 1961.

Harzfeld's was again represented in the presence of a president several months later. The Specialty Stores Association (SSA), started in 1921, was a cooperative of over a dozen specialty stores throughout the country. It had offices on both coasts that would assist buyers on their trips. In April 1961, the SSA met in Kansas City. Lester Siegel Sr. arranged for a tour of the Truman Library in Independence, where the group met the former president and viewed the recently unveiled Thomas Hart Benton mural.[51] Mr. Siegel and the former president shared in the commissioning of the artist for their respective murals. The work at the library was entitled *Independence and the Opening of the West*. Unlike the Harzfeld's mural, this was painted on-site, directly on the walls of the lobby. Many of the same techniques as employed in *Achelous and Hercules* in 1947—such as extensive research, clay maquettes studies and live models—were again used in this mural. Benton was assisted by Charles Banks Wilson, an artist from Oklahoma, in executing the multiple panels.

After World War I and throughout the 1940s, the area employed over four thousand persons and boasted that one out of every seven women in the

Above: Harzfeld's Corinth store, Prairie Village, Kansas, 1963.

Below: The Petticoat Lane location featured these bright pink corset chairs in the lingerie department in 1964, when the fourth floor was remodeled and made "pink & feminine." These came up for sale in a now closed store in Mission, Kansas, several years ago.

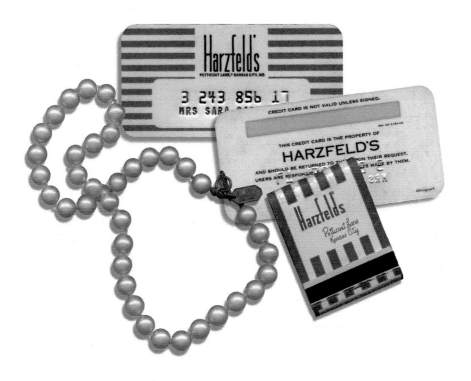

Above: Credit cards, pearls and matches all with Harzfeld's branding, circa 1960s.

Left: Door handles from Harzfeld's Corinth store as a condensed "H." Enhanced photo.

Cover illustration by Patricia George featuring Norell fashion. *Courtesy of* The Independent, *October 23, 1965.*

United States purchased a Kansas City–made garment. Manufacturing of garments was the second largest employer of any industry in Kansas City. The industry adopted a "section system," by which workers specialized in a specific task, such as sewing a zipper. This allowed for greater growth in adding untrained workers.[52]

Chapter 9

Seasons of Change

L ester Siegel Jr. began his career at the company by working part time in the shipping department as a teenager. He later took on a variety of executive responsibilities after obtaining his BA from Carleton College and a master's in business administration from Harvard University Business School.

Siegel tells of becoming friends with Thomas Hart Benton and his wife, Rita. On a Sunday evening in the early '60s, Lester invited the couple and a group of friends over to his apartment near the Country Club Plaza for a chili dinner. Everyone had a great time listening to music and doing the current dance craze. Benton sketched the lively scene and later painted a work entitled *Doing the Twist.* Just like his father, Siegel developed an affinity for the artist's work.[53]

Lester Jr. became the third president of Harzfeld's in 1966, the seventy-fifth anniversary year of the store. His father maintained a close relationship with the store and served as board chairman.[54] The commemorative year was an opportunity to look both forward with new leadership and also back in time to the store's origins. Two ladies representing the store assumed Victorian dress to bring awareness to the diamond anniversary celebration, and they visited local businesses and organizations with gifts of champagne. The fourteen firms visited were Rothschild's, Emery Bird Thayer, Duff and Repp, Woolf Brothers, Jenkins, the *Kansas City Star,* Macy's, Shukert's, the Jones Store, Wolferman's, Jaccard's, the Palace, Adler's and *The Independent.*

Lester Siegel Jr., president of Harzfeld's, circa 1960s.

Lorene Roberson started her time with the store at the Plaza location, and later she became assistant manager at the Corinth store in Prairie Village, Kansas. She shares her thoughts about the Harzfeld's dress code: "If you weren't wearing pantyhose, you were sent home. We all wore the beehive hairdo when it was in vogue, and dress lengths were also followed. You were the background for fashion. They were so up on the seasons, the day after Christmas, all display windows switched over to resort wear."[55]

In 1966, Lorene was promoted to buyer of coats and suits, having six stores to buy for. On buying trips to New York lasting between one to three weeks, she might attend four or five fashion shows per day. "We were high fashion…it [the merchandise] had to come in quickly," states Roberson.

When a two-level, forty-thousand-square-foot location was created for the new Metcalf South Mall in Overland Park, Kansas, in 1967, Roberson became Harzfeld's first female store manager. She was excited about the new opportunity and was able to hire a wonderful new staff of one hundred employees. The store had a gift shop, beauty salon and offered shoe repair. Its French Room featured a six-hundred-pound antique chandelier obtained through Jack Rees Interiors, which handled the décor of the store. The hand-chased chandelier was said to have been presented by Queen Victoria to the Soldiers and Sailors Club of London.[56]

Harzfeld's president Lester Siegel Jr. married Myra Bailey Epstein of Dallas, Texas, on July 27, 1968. Myra was with Neiman Marcus in Dallas, where the company originated in 1907.

In 1968, legendary Emery Bird Thayer, a historic department store east of and across the street from Harzfeld's on Petticoat Lane, closed after 105 years of business. The large Victorian building was razed three years later. This was a sign that downtown Kansas City was losing ground to the

Seventy-fifth-anniversary collage including an ad for the *Kansas City Star*; an announcement designed by Erasmus Beall; a perfumed cachet given to customers; a photo of Richard B. Fowler (president of the *Kansas City Star*) being presented with champagne by two women representing Harzfeld's in Victorian dress; and a thank-you letter to the store from fashion designer Adele Simpson.

Left: Back cover
illustration by Patricia
George for Adele
Simpson fashion. The
Independent, *January 7,
1967.*

Below: Metcalf South
Harzfeld's illustration of
entrance, 1967.

Original cover illustration by Patricia George of Malcolm Starr fashions suggested to be worn to the Performing Arts Foundation's production of *Orpheus in the Underworld*. The Independent, *May 13, 1967.*

Above: Jack Rees interior sketch for French Room, lower level, Metcalf South Harzfeld's, Overland Park, Kansas, 1967.

Below: Back cover advertisement featuring a model sketched at Jack Rees Interiors, welcoming the members of the American Institute of Decorators (AID) to their conference. Illustration by Patricia George featuring tank and trouser by Ole Borden for Rembrandt. *Courtesy of* The Independent, *April 19, 1967.*

Left: Original fashion illustration by Patricia George of Mao jacket and paneled skirt by Bill Blass for Maurice Rentner. The Independent, *February 10, 1968.*

Below: Jack Rees interior sketch for Metcalf South Harzfeld's, 1967.

There were numerous covers that were done in partnership, some of which promoted local events. Copy pertaining to the cover reads: "The romance of evening black, absolutely elegant from attending the premiere benefit performance of the 'Medea' May 17th, sponsored by the Performing Arts Foundation. Left, flounces of fluted silk chiffon create a whimsical aura at 170.00. Right, tri-dimensional designs dot airy marquisette over a muted nude background, 140.00. French Room, third [floor] Downtown and Plaza." *Courtesy of* The Independent, *May 11, 1968.*

suburban shopping developments, and Harzfeld's was relying more on its branch stores than previously.

Two stores saw big change in '71. Blue Ridge was originally built as an open-air mall, but by the summer of 1971 it was enclosed, which became part of a promotion called "The Great Cover Up." A fire at the Columbia store necessitated a move from 922 East Broadway to 16 North Tenth Street.

The '70s were a time to say goodbye to a number of Harzfeld's associates and friends. Lester Siegel Sr. passed away on June 9, 1971, at the age of seventy-seven. He was survived by his wife, Frieda, who died on October 6, 1978. Thomas Hart Benton left us in January 1975, and Harzfeld's claim to baseball fame, Casey Stengel, passed in September of the same year.

Original cover illustration by Patricia George of an Adele Simpson fashion. The Independent, *August 30, 1969.*

Original cover illustration by Patricia George of a Chester Weinberg fashion. The Independent, *December 5, 1970.*

Another connection to Harzfeld's was made evident after another passing. President Harry S Truman passed away on December 26, 1972. When items from the Truman home in Independence, Missouri, were being inventoried in 1981, the first letters found, sent from President Truman to Bess during World War I, were in a giant green and white striped box from Harzfeld's. It was said that "most everything was in Harzfeld's boxes or bags."[57] The letters were later published in the book *Dear Bess*, by Dr. Robert H. Ferrell. Bess Truman passed away on October 18, 1982.

In February 1972, the store was acquired by Garfinckel, Brooks Brothers, Miller & Rhoads, Inc.[58] Harzfeld's had gone public in 1959,[59] which may have rendered the "friendly" acquisition feasible. The new ownership had greater capital and began looking for ways to expand the chain of six stores. In 1974, the parent company purchased two Gus Mayer stores in Oklahoma:[60] one in Penn Square Mall in Oklahoma City's well-to-do north side and the other at the Utica Square shopping center in Tulsa.

The Tulsa location found a famous customer in the actress Loretta Young. Her daughter-in-law, Linda, tells of their visits:

Loretta and I enjoyed many shopping expeditions at the Harzfeld's at Utica Square in Tulsa. Loretta came to visit us in Tulsa and stayed for about six months. Of course, I introduced her to my favorite store and it became her favorite as well. She bought several cocktail dresses, shoes, handbags and loads of other accessories at the store. She liked the selection of formal wear and she enjoyed the blouse and casual wear department too! We would spend hours there and I have great memories of shopping with her.

At the time, I was the promotions director at Tulsa radio station KRAV-FM96 and my husband was a news reporter for KTUL-TV (ABC). We

*were in the public eye and attended many social events, and I was usually
wearing something from Harzfeld's!*

*The Harzfeld's staff was wonderful, the clothing selections and the
styles were top of the line. It was always a pleasure to walk in the door of
the store.*

Another connection Harzfeld's had to Tulsa, Oklahoma, was through
Siegmund Harzfeld's nephew, Joseph Leslie Seidenbach. After working at
Harzfeld's, Seidenbach moved to Tulsa after a visit in 1916.[61] He opened
his own store near First and Main Streets. "Seidenbach's New Store," an
impressive Gothic-style building, was erected at 413–415 South Main in
1927. Sadly, it was demolished after the store closed in the mid-1960s.[62]

Catalogues from the '70s sometimes featured photos shot in exotic locations
such as Bavaria, Portugal or aboard a Norwegian Caribbean Lines ship.
Models such as Shelley Hack in a cable-knit sweater dress or Cheryl Tiegs in
an Antron nylon swim suit would occasionally show up in the pages.

On August 29, 1977, Harzfeld's held the *Vogue* Fall Collection Fashion
Show to benefit the Historic Kansas City Foundation. This was the second
fashion show the store orchestrated to benefit the organization. Harzfeld's
display windows featured Kansas City's architectural heritage. The proceeds
helped preserve an 1888 colonial revival house on Gillham Road that still
stands today.[63]

Less than one month later, Harzfeld's and most all businesses on the Country
Club Plaza were presented with their own renovation projects. Sixteen
inches of rain fell on September 12, causing severe flooding throughout the
shopping district. The basement level of Harzfeld's was in complete ruins.
The damage prompted a renovation of the store. One fortunate aspect of
the flood was that Harzfeld's stored its furs in a downtown warehouse. Many
other stores lost their inventory and customers' furs that were in storage.
That fall, Harzfeld's had strong fur sales, as many customers were replacing
those articles destroyed through other stores in the flood.

Lester Siegel Jr. retired as president of Harzfeld's in June 1978. It was
the end of an eighty-seven-year direct relationship that the Siegel family
shared with the specialty store.[64] On the occasion of his retirement, Lester Jr.
observed in the *Kansas City Times*, "I guess certainly the biggest change, not
only for us but for all retailers, has been the decline in downtown business
and the rapid expansion of the suburbs since the mid-1950s. I feel Harzfeld's
was one of the very first to take advantage of that expansion since we went
to the Plaza in 1954."

Above, left: Cover illustration by Mary Louise Wilson. *Courtesy of* The Independent, *May 5, 1979.*

Above, right: Power suit from Harzfeld's catalogue, circa 1980.

A few months later, in September, Anne Stegner was named the first female president of the firm. The store continued its prestigious status, but more change was yet to come. The downtown location was suffering.[65] In February 1980, David Layne was named president.[66] In November 1981, Allied Stores acquired the store chain as part of its takeover of Garfinckel, Brooks Brothers, Miller & Rhoads, Inc.[67]

Harzfeld's had a tradition of being the target of cupid's arrow, and this held true to the end. John Schinkel worked at Harzfeld's for over seven years, and it was there he met his wife, Kim. He was the receiving manager at Blue Ridge, then at the downtown store (opening it for business every morning in the early '80s) and finally at the Metcalf location. Kim started with seasonal work, which led to switchboard operations downtown and then an executive

Calvin Klein jeans and corduroys from Harzfeld's catalogue, circa 1980. Years prior, the store offered his early faux fur coat line.

Henry Moore's Sheep Piece is the scene for models showing off fashions from HARZFELDS by designer Perry Ellis. The four-ton Berlin-cast bronze graces the mall south of the Nelson Gallery.

Left: Harzfeld's ad in a 1981 Folly Theater program. The two models in Perry Ellis fashions posed with, and quite inappropriately on, a familiar Kansas City sculpture. *Henry Moore, English (1898–1986)*. Sheep Piece, *1971–1972. Bronze, height: 168 inches. The Kansas City Sculpture Park at the Nelson-Atkins Museum of Art. Board of Parks and Recreation Commissioners, Gift of N. Clyde Degginger.*

Below: Group photo of 125 Harzfeld's associates outside the Plaza location, circa early 1980s. *Courtesy of Roy Albin Jr.*

Collage of Harzfeld's branded items from authors' collection, with the addition of the bag holder from the collection of Gary and Elaine Kabrick.

secretary position for the president and executives. They married in December 1981. The ladies of the Blue Ridge store were absolutely in seventh heaven to think that their matchmaking skills had proven so remarkable! There were more people from Harzfeld's at the wedding than there were of their other friends and relatives, so they often refer to it as "the Harzfeld's Wedding."

Both John and Kim were there until the end, when the company was closed down in 1984. Kim remembers making the move of the headquarters to 8900 Ward Parkway in early 1984 from the downtown offices:

> *It was announced that Allied Stores of New York was* [pulling] *their corporate support, and that* [therefore] *Harzfeld's could no longer survive as a corporate entity. Soon, the offices that had recently buzzed with activity now gathered dust; sales figures dwindled to nothing...It became clear that I couldn't get on at Bonwit Teller. Sadly, all that would remain of Harzfeld's would be warm memories of working with an extended (and somewhat eccentric) family, and being a part of a very special place in the history of Kansas City retail.*
>
> *From time to time, I encounter one of the old green-and-white boxes, or someone who used to shop there. It seems difficult NOT to smile at the warmth that builds in my heart at that moment.*

Chapter 10

The End of an Era

The once-pioneering specialty store downtown on Petticoat Lane closed its doors to the public early in 1984. The location that once boasted thousands of shoppers on its streets and at one time was known as a mecca for the elegant and fashion-conscious woman was quiet. The now-famous mural *Achelous and Hercules*, by Thomas Hart Benton, found a new home at the Smithsonian American Art Museum in Washington, D.C.

The Blue Ridge location had closed late in '83 and the other branches closed in the summer of '84; the flagship location at the Plaza was the only holdout. By this time, Donald Falk had become president, and he announced in August that the Plaza Harzfeld's would be closing as well. The location was converted to a Bonwit Teller store on November 10, 1984.

The store closings were a result of changing retail trends and an extremely complicated chain of events set into motion on Wall Street. Motivated by fees, financial institutions financed highly leveraged buyouts of retail conglomerates. This led to the collapse of many stores and the loss of thousands of jobs in the late '80s.

Canadian developer Robert Campeau, through the Campeau Corporation, purchased Allied Corporation in a highly leveraged buyout.[68] In an attempt to pay off debts assumed through this purchase, the Bonwit Teller chain was sold off in 1987. The purchase of Bonwit Teller by Australian developer L.J. Hooker was also highly leveraged. The Campeau Corporation then acquired Federated Department Stores in 1988 in yet another buyout. In 1989, both Campeau Corporation and L.J. Hooker declared bankruptcy.

Petticoat Lane, Kansas City, Missouri. Digital photo montage creating a classic view looking east from Main, fall 2009.

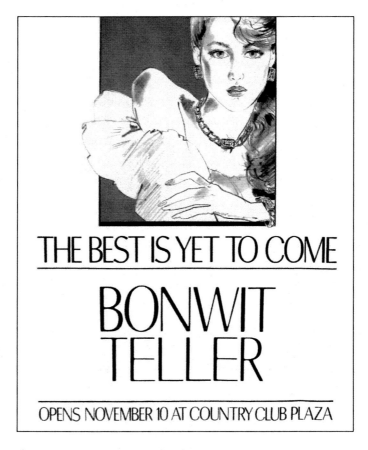

THE BEST IS YET TO COME

BONWIT TELLER

OPENS NOVEMBER 10 AT COUNTRY CLUB PLAZA

Courtesy of The Independent, *November 1, 1984.*

The bankruptcy caused the Bonwit Teller on the Country Club Plaza to close in the summer of 1990. The store had approximately sixty-eight full-time and twenty-five part-time employees.[69]

Although the downtown location of Harzfeld's was closed in early 1984, the building that it called home was spared the wrecking ball. The store's façade was secured and returned to its original appearance in a renovation that was part of the Town Pavilion development, completed in 1988. This development also saved the historic Boley building on the corner of Twelfth and Walnut. Revitalization of downtown Kansas City seems to be taking hold today. Efforts made over twenty years ago have helped to preserve our history and establish a foothold for the improvements we are currently witnessing. Kansas City has fertile ground for the future and will continue to show the world what's up to date.

Chapter 11

Stories and Recollections

Following are stories told by or about associates of Harzfeld's.

ARTHUR AND AMELIA KABRICK,
SHARED BY THEIR SONS ARTHUR AND GARY

Amelia Borchert admired the position her aunt Lucinda held at Harzfeld's. With her connection, she, along with her sister Margaret, was able to secure positions at the store. When prompted for proof of her age, she was able to skirt the issue for two years, until she turned sixteen. At that point, most of her fellow employees assumed that she was eighteen years old, including Arthur Kabrick Jr., who started sending her flirtatious notes at work. Their relationship blossomed into love. With surprise at the eventual revelation of her age, the relationship continued. Once she was eighteen, they eloped in 1930, unbeknownst to their families. It was rumored they may have been married on their lunch hour from the store.

Amelia left Harzfeld's shortly after having Arthur III in 1933. On a visit back to the store a few years later, Amelia and Margaret brought young Arthur with them to visit their friends and rode up the crowded elevator with Mr. Harzfeld to the tenth floor. As little Arthur reached for the lever arm after the elevator stopped, Sieg exclaimed "No, no!" in concern for the child's safety.[70]

Arthur Jr. was consistently assuming new positions and responsibilities. He had been involved in buying, clerical, became floor manager, worked in the tabulating room, supervisor, assistant to the controller and eventually controller. Arthur worked there until 1946; a total of twenty-one years.[71]

Columbia store shoe ad with illustration by New York cartoonist Alan Dunn (1900–1974). *Columbia Missourian*, November, 14, 1937.

WARREN DALTON

Warren Dalton, born in 1917, enjoyed his time as manager of the shoe department at the Harzfeld's in Columbia. He was hired away from JC Penney in early 1938. He remembers traveling to Kansas City and had a chance to meet with Lester Siegel Sr. and Sieg Harzfeld. He remembered that Sieg was quite short in stature. He also fondly remembers the managers of the Columbia locations, Leo and Lois Van Coutren, "the Vans."

With its connections in Kansas City, it was *the* store for shoes in Columbia. He was able to offer brands and styles that weren't available elsewhere. His customers included students and their parents from the University of Missouri-Columbia, Stephens and Christian College (now Columbia College). Shoes could be sent from Kansas City by bus in the matter of one or two days when needed.

After obtaining his degree from the University of Missouri, he thought about pursuing a law degree, but found that retail was possibly more lucrative at that time. He was very satisfied with his 8 percent commission on the $40,000 of sales for 1938. After leaving the store in 1940, he managed another ladies' store, and later owned Suzanne's in Columbia.

He is the author of *It is Never Too Late*, an autobiographical book in which he shares many life lessons. He also writes a column for the *Columbia Daily Tribune*.[72]

BESSIE WOLF, AS TOLD BY HER GRANDDAUGHTER, JUDY MENDELSOHN LANES

Bessie Wolf began her career at Harzfeld's in 1910 at an early age and continued through 1984. She was an institution and only took off two times in her life, never a vacation because she had to make money. She took off for the birth of her first daughter, Pauline Frances, and then again when she had another daughter, my mother, Helen Felice.

You could find her on the fifth floor in the children's department every day, except on Sunday and during the Jewish holidays. She told her daughters, "Don't have your children during 'my busy season.'" That meant the holidays, and none of us were born then, either. We still laugh about that today and I tell friends and people at the office: "No, not now, it's my 'busy season.'"

Bessie dressed four or five generations of little girls. Many still remember Miss Wolf at Harzfeld's to this day! She was a tiny little woman with impeccable grooming habits; a "uniform" of navy blue, black and beige dresses, and suits for winter and spring/summer, because in those days they dressed to go to work and were proud to be Harzfeld's employees. She always had a twinkle in her eye and was grateful to those who bought from her…it was commission only. Her job and her daughters were the only things in her life and sometimes my aunt and mother would laugh and say, it was Harzfeld's only!

She brought half a sandwich for lunch each day and would stand behind the enclosed area in the back and take a bite or two, always peering out the little peephole in the swinging door to see if someone needed help. She kept a diary of everyone she sold to…maybe not a lot, sometimes great sales, but in her book she had their size, what styles they liked and of course their parents' names and addresses. Some were from out of town like Tulsa, Oklahoma, or St. Joseph, Missouri, and just a day's ride away. Often she would write cards telling them about upcoming sales and a dress that just came in that "little Trish" might like to see. She had a desk in her living room at home where she would write those famous notes and Christmas cards showing her appreciation that I have today and my youngest niece has already put "dibs on" when I die.

I remember walking into the first floor and seeing jewelry; second floor was where I really had to behave and act like a lady. There were live models who would model the clothes that my mother would buy for herself. The mezzanine was where the restrooms were, and finally, when we got to the fifth floor, the man who ran the elevator in his crisp dark uniform and white gloves would pull open the door and announce, "Fifth floor, girls seven to fourteen, infants and shoes." We had arrived, ah…Grandma's floor.

I also remember "fashion shows" for the seasons. We, the grandchildren, nieces, friends, daughters and sons, were the models and were paid five dollars per outfit and five dollars per store. That was when Blue Ridge and the Plaza store opened. It was quite a lot of money and I was so happy that I would sometimes purchase the clothes that I modeled.

While working for Hallmark Cards, we had to tell stories about Christmas and what we love. Mine was always the same…I loved the shiny wrapped packages that Grandma would carry into our house for the day because they had the most beautiful paper, ribbons and enhancements on them that I had ever seen. Sometimes I really didn't even care what was in them, it was just wonderful to see all the packages.

I remember during the fall when it was time for my annual trek to the eye doctor, we would go downtown in the morning so we could watch the American Royal Parade. We would open the windows that were in the fitting rooms so we could all see the parade pass by. My eyes were dilated, so I bet my memories were more vivid than most.

Our memories of Harzfeld's still ring true because I still have those beautiful enameled green and white boxes forever tucked in my closet, as do many women in Kansas City.

Upon Grandma's death, she left her beloved Harzfeld's twenty-five-year pin, with diamonds, pearls, rubies and sapphires, to my mother, Helen. Upon her death in 2004, I took it to the only granddaughter who works retail. She is a human relations director at a national chain store in Atlanta, Georgia. I felt Grandma would have loved that![73]

ROSINA JUSTINA (WALZ) MCKAY, SHARED BY HER GREAT-NIECE JOLYNNE (WALZ) MARTINEZ

Rosina Justina (Walz) McKay was a furrier for Harzfeld's from at least 1930 until sometime before her early death in 1948. The daughter of impoverished German immigrants, it was a major life change for her to go from living in poverty to selling furs to wealthy ladies at Harzfeld's.

She also did some comparison shopping for Harzfeld's, scoping out the competition's merchandise and prices, and when she saw something of good quality at a good price, she would snap it up. She never had children of her own, but her nieces were always well dressed when they were girls, despite the years of the Depression and World War II.[74]

BERTHA HELLMAN, AS TOLD BY HER SON, LLOYD HELLMAN

Bertha Hellman became a changed woman as a result of getting a job at Harzfeld's.

First, she was overweight as was customary for women of the 1920s. After all, the Czar was said to have kicked any woman out of his bed under two hundred pounds. When she reduced some sixty pounds (amphetamine

I'd bet from a licensed MD), it was then she started looking for a job and found it at Harzfeld's. She was still somewhat of a stout woman with ample breasts, but had a carriage about her and a jovial personality that was winning.

She was in the lingerie department on the fourth floor. One of the first things she did, when she started in 1944, was consult her coworkers in the foundation department to be fitted by the experts to make her as shapely as possible.

In those days, retail stores serviced their customers by "showing" them what merchandise might appeal to them after searching out the right size. My mom was such a saleslady. "Salesclerk" was a slight pejorative and not appropriate for high-class Harzfeld's. Robes and nightgowns were the high-ticket items followed by slips, panties and the like.

When my mother caught a bride to be, who had the money to shop at Harzfeld's, that was a bonanza for her day. A robe or two (consistent with the season), two or three silk nightgowns (yes, even black ones), panties and brassieres to size. There were fitting rooms to which the goodies were brought to be selected by the bride and usually her mother. A buying bride could consume two or three hours in selecting her trousseau.

But the best time of year for the on-commission sales staff was pre-Christmas. Gentlemen of quality, in their suits (vest) and ties, came to the fourth floor, took off their overcoats and sat in front of the low wood and leather (as I remember) counter (not wholly of glass), while my mom and her co-employees draped dressing gowns and nightgowns (and later silk pajamas) over the counter for them to appraise. Larger gowns she held up to herself to show; smaller gowns she called over a smaller salesperson so she could hold the item up to them. Men were the easy pickins' because they were out of their element, were slightly embarrassed, had no time and wanted to get the hell out of there. $100 to $200 robes were at the top of the line and flew off the shelves, particularly on Christmas Eve day.

My mother was the number two best saleslady during her most productive days. Mrs. Bernstein was far and away the best lingerie saleslady. She had a "following" and predated my mom's hiring by some years. On those occasions when mom had a better sales day than Mrs. Bernstein, we heard about it at dinner that night. Harzfeld's money that my mom earned was important to our family. My dad was a paperhanger and painter and work was always spotty, particularly in the winter when sales were pretty good at Harzfeld's.

My dad died at age fifty-six (1951), at which time my mom was fifty-one. I can tell you, that job at Harzfeld's was an emotional and financial godsend. I graduated from the University of Missouri-Columbia that June and went into the Marine Corps, so the job was all she had and it served her well.

I too worked at Harzfeld's, on the fourth floor in the play-shoe department Thursday nights and summers, from my senior year in high school until I went into the service.

J.J. Jaffee was the "buyer" for the shoe department, which was the largest and most beautifully stocked west of Mississippi, or possibly in the country. Prices ran from high to exorbitant. The biggest seller for many years was a platform sling pump with a small western belt tip that belted the instep, by Palter Deliso, the high end of the Deliso Deb supplier. This shoe, carried in about six colors, was finally copied by Bakers shoe stores, but they weren't Palters. Jaffee traveled to New York and Paris to buy shoes and often suggested changes of design for the shoes he selected for his department. He was short, wore tweedy suits and Bay Rum cologne. He insisted that the shoebox be opened carefully in front of the customer and that the precious shoe be presented "like a jewel."

Finally, I looked at the Thomas Hart Benton painting over the elevators every morning that I came to work at the store. I loved it and recognized that Harzfeld's was a classy store for having that fine piece of art on its wall.[75]

MERRY CHRISTMAS, HARRY

In 1919, after returning from World War I, Harry and his army buddy, Eddie, opened a haberdashery (men's store) two blocks from Harzfeld's at 104 West Twelfth Street. In late 1946, the employees of Harzfeld's created a giant scroll to wish Harry, now the thirty-third president of the United States, and his family a Merry Christmas. It was signed by all the employees. In a letter dated December 28, 1946, President Harry S Truman thanked everyone at Harzfeld's and stated, "It is the longest Christmas card I have ever received."

Bridal ad prepared by Carl Reimers Co., Inc., New York. *Brides*, autumn 1952.

DROLETTE (BRADLEY) WEIDEMAN

Drolette (Bradley) Weideman modeled for the French Room (which included couture and "better dresses") on the third floor, and also provided bridal help when needed.

Miss Vivian Carnes was the buyer. She let me go into the stock room and pick out what I wanted to put on. Very special clothes in those days. The favorite salesperson would go in back, get the clothes and show them [to the prospective buyer]. *I would be available to help wherever I might be needed.*

I thoroughly enjoyed it. We had a floor man, Dan Lehane, on duty all the time. He just basically was in his coat and tie, stood there and was available [to the customer]. *He'd greet Mrs. Jones: "I'll call Mrs. Pepperdine for you, please have a seat." He knew their names, and it was his responsibility to greet them and seat them. It was an era of service.*

It was just a wonderful, wonderful atmosphere. [Both] *in terms of service, and everything was carpeted and lovely.*

[It was] *very much a close relationship between the customer and the saleslady on the floor. Almost like a doctor—you'd go to your saleslady.*

The third floor was connected to the bridal department. Through Mrs. Delaney (the bridal buyer at that time), I would help get the bride dressed at the church, look after the bridesmaids' dresses and make sure the wedding went smoothly. Nowadays you hire these people; but in those days, the store provided the service.

I spent the day putting several things on. I was the right size. Vivian wouldn't want you to wear something that a client had already bought. She would suggest something [to maintain a certain item's exclusivity or a client's privacy].

It just points out that they were very alert to pleasing and keeping their customers happy. Miss Carnes knew everybody—she was there for years—her buying was very much bent toward doing what she felt she could sell. In those days, she did a remarkable business. She would buy with her customers' likes and tastes in mind, instead of buying what the designers were making and trying to make it work. She knew her clientele.

There's just not another store like Harzfeld's. It's just special.[76]

Harzfeld's 1953 Distinguished Merit Awards, presented by Lester Siegel Sr. to Vivian Carnes (French Room) and Jay Jaffee (shoes).

SUZANNE DRYER

As Drolette had done for years before her, Suzanne Dryer modeled the fashions in the late sixties. She recalls that training on how to treat customers lasted nearly a week. She learned that everyone should be treated as if they were well-to-do regardless of any outward appearance. This held true when a seemingly poorly dressed customer revealed fine handmade undergarments from France.

Suzanne recalled the pneumatic tube system that was in use for handling cash transactions. The funds to purchase a garment were inserted into a small container that was whisked away to a money handler and shot back with any change to be returned to the customers. This system remained in place until the end at the Petticoat Lane store.

When not in the French Room, Suzanne would work in the junior department. They were able to wear the fashions on the floor on

Saturdays. She recalls pantsuits and one of her favorite items, the Diane Von Furstenberg wrap dress. At thirty-five dollars, it was an item she aspired to own. She was able to purchase two outfits per season, at one third off.

Vivian Carnes and J.J. Jaffee Receive Awards

On December 17, 1953, Mr. Siegel presented Distinguished Merit Awards to Vivian Carnes, French Room buyer, and Jay J. Jaffee, shoe buyer. Mr. Siegel said,

> *I am happy to present two awards this year. The first to Miss Carnes, whose untiring efforts have built Harzfeld's fashion reputation in our community. Her taste, fabulous energy—often in the face of seemingly unsurmountable* [sic] *situations—have resulted in establishing a name in the fashion field second to none. Her 'know how' and good judgment have made her an outstanding success with customers, personnel and management.*
>
> *Mr. Jaffee, the second recipient, has brought national shoe fame to Petticoat Lane. From 1927, the time he started buying footwear for Harzfeld's, he has gradually established this institution as a fashion show center. Harzfeld's name, together with his, have become synonymous in the shoe industry. His style sense and forecasting ability are famous. His advice and judgment are sought after and his capabilities envied and admired by competitors, manufacturers and stylists. His daring and sense of sell are notorious.*

Bernadine Glynn

Bernadine, a talented seamstress, was the manager of the downtown alteration shop. She worked on the floor with Vivian Carnes and close working relationships with the customers in the French Room. The following is from the *Twenties Tooter*, a one-time tabloid for the January 27, 1961 Twenty-five-Year Club's Roaring Twenties party, at which Bernadine was inducted, along with four other ladies:

Bernadine Glynn, manager of the Downtown Alteration Shop, is renowned for her Irish wit and fashionplate appearance. Her favorite pastimes—when she can find a few leisure moments at home—are reading or concocting delicious "eatables." She has the traditional "green thumb," too. Ever see her botanical garden in the Alterations Shop? Given a few "sprouts" from June Conrad's African violets, Bernadine transformed them into a lush, big family of blossoming plants. These were presented to various store departments at Christmas. We notice that, already, one-by-one the pots of violets are being returned to Green-Thumb Glynn for revival!

MARY JANE KRUGH

I worked at Harzfeld's as an assistant buyer in the Petticoat Lane Dress Shop during the mid-1950s. I grew up in Independence, Missouri, and still lived there when I started my first and only job. The morning and evening trip by public transportation was pleasant for me as I made acquaintances with many people as I rode to the job I grew to love.

Mr. Siegel was a peach and admired by all his employees. I first started in the business office, doing clerical work outside of his office. That was a plus because he knew me by face, probably not by name at that time. After a year of office work, the merchandise manager, Morris Schlanger, called me to his office one day to tell me I was being considered for the job of assistant buyer, was I interested? I was not sure if I would be capable, but he assured me he would be there to assist me if I needed it. I accepted the promotion. My maiden name was Mary Jane Simpson, Mr. Schlanger's initials were the same as mine—he was Morris Jacob Schlanger—so he often referred to me as M.J.S. or "daughter!"

During my tenure as an assistant buyer, I made two trips to New York with the buyers and one trip alone to California. I will never forget my first view of the New York skyscrapers as we flew into that exciting city. The buyer I worked under was Pat Judd. She showed me the ropes, plus we stayed in an apartment on Park Avenue owned by one of her friends.

We were treated so graciously by everyone in the office of the Specialty Store Association, offering us Broadway show tickets and great business and restaurant contacts. What a wonderful way to see New York City for the first time.

One day I left Harzfeld's for lunch and walked around the corner to Wolferman's. At that time it was a very upscale grocery, bakery, deli and had a small lunch counter on the first floor, a few tables on the balcony, a large rectangular lunch counter on the lower level and a lovely large, pleasant dining room on the upper level. That was the Tiffin Room. I took the elevators to the lower-floor lunch counter. As I stepped off the elevator, I took the first available spot I saw, sat down and ordered my lunch. The male person next to me attempted to start a conversation about what I had chosen for lunch. I barely glanced at him as I replied to his questions in as few words as possible. He asked where I worked. I told him the sixth floor of Harzfeld's…nothing more…finished lunch and left.

I took the next day (a Saturday) off, which was unusual in the retail business but was at home when I answered a phone call and it was the man from Wolferman's! I was astounded that someone I had a brief encounter with at lunch now had my name and phone number. How could this happen? I later learned he called the personnel office with a wild story of a purchase he had made and desperately needed to speak to me about it.

He was given my name and phone number. He had the nerve to invite me out on a date. Of course I said NO and asked him not to call again, assuming I would never hear from him again. However, the next week I received a call from him at work, again asking me to have lunch with him. The answer was still NO! The next week he called again (at work) suggesting we have lunch. This time I agreed assuming it would be safe in a restaurant with lots of people around, also a free lunch, and I could make it plain to him I wasn't going to go out with him—then I realized I didn't remember what he looked like. He said he would meet me on the first floor of Harzfeld's near the elevator. I asked two people to ride down the elevator with me and look carefully at the person I was meeting; in case I didn't return, they could identify my abductor!

Lorie Newhouse was the merchandise manager of the accessory department on the first floor and had started a conversation with this young man who was hanging around the elevators but never got on. He learned his name and place of business just as I stepped off the elevator. His name was John A. Krugh and his family's real estate office was in the Altman building at Eleventh and Walnut.

John suggested we again have lunch at Wolferman's—but this time we took the elevator up to the lovely Tiffin Room. Over lunch, which was very pleasant, we discovered we had a few mutual friends. I decided he really was not at all weird and scary as I imagined. When lunch was over, he asked for the check and a pen to sign it. Hmm! No one I had dated had a charge account in a restaurant! He again asked me out and I said I would think about it. I was impressed with his flawless manners. He walked back with me to Harzfeld's. I safely returned to my place of work and later I learned from him, he dashed back to the Tiffin Room and explained he was there to pay for the lunches he had just signed for, because he had no charge account there but was hoping to impress me! We lunched in the Tiffin Room many times after that. The staff knew of his intentions and always gave us special service...I accepted real dates and a year and a half later, we were married. Some of my single friends at Harzfeld's would tell us they were eating at Wolferman's each day in hopes of finding someone like John. I continued working at Harzfeld's until my first child was born two years later. My husband John passed away four years ago but throughout our forty-seven years of marriage, he would often say he often wondered where we would be if I hadn't worked at Harzfeld's and we both had not eaten at Wolferman's.[77]

John G. Cate

I joined Harzfeld's in 1970 as merchandise manager for fashion accessories, cosmetics, intimate apparel and children's. I previously worked at the Higbee Co. in Cleveland, Ohio, and the J.L. Hudson Co. in Detroit, Michigan. What a great experience to work at this fine store, under the tutelage of Maurice Breyer (general merchandise manager) and Morris Schlanger (divisional merchandise manager of apparel). I think the two had about eighty years of experience at Harzfeld's. I stayed until 1977, then left to join Levy's, a Federated store in Tucson, Arizona.

I remember the great Christmas windows with the animated displays... what a joy! They reminded me of the Christmas windows that Higbee's was famous for (and were shown in the classic A Christmas Story).

It was a great group to work with...I have so many good memories of my seven years. Several European buying trips, endless trips to New York and Dallas...it was like a family![78]

ESSIE MARSHALL, AS TOLD BY HER GRANDDAUGHTER, DR. DEBORAH STEPHENS

Harzfeld's has a very special place in my heart. My grandmother worked at Harzfeld's for twenty-six years on the sixth floor. All of my baby clothes, back-to-school clothes, prom dresses, etc. came from this great store. I have many of her hatboxes, hats and other items I have saved and collected over the years.

I can still remember the beautiful mural and the smell of Estee Lauder as you entered the revolving door. What great memories![79]

Sweater bar at the Plaza Harzfeld's, 1954.

Rose (the) Hunter, by Lorene Roberson

I had taken my turn as room mother, den mother, PTA and etc. I now wanted to return to the "working world." To work short hours seemed reasonable. I would be home the hours my sons, Mac and Jac, were out of school.

I applied for employment at the Plaza Harzfeld's Store. I was hired for part-time sales at the sweater bar.

The bar was near the French Room. Stools at the bar were frequently used by idle salespeople, waiting for their next customer.

One such person was Rose Hunter. Her clientele were Kansas City's society women. Rose was always attractively dressed, in her forties—with a very large bosom.

She knew fashion, and they knew she knew. She was very popular.

On this particular day, Rose was seated at the bar. I was ready to write a sales ticket (we did that in 1955). Frustrated, I blurted, "No pen, again, borrowed as usual!" "Here, use this one" said Rose, as she pulled a pen from her bosom, and handed it to me.

At another time, I needed a piece of paper to write on. None available, but Rose, from her ample bosom, gave me a small note pad. "Rose," I asked, "if I wanted a hot cup of coffee, I wouldn't be surprised if you couldn't provide it." She answered, smiling, "With cream?" She always left one laughing.[80]

Roy Albin

Roy Albin started in 1978 and worked until the stores closed in 1984. During this time, there were a number of transitions in leadership and changes in the stores.

Lester Jr. had retired by the time I got there. Saul Kass worked there and I remember David Layne. Then they brought in an operations VP, Dick Bowen, originally from Filene's.

I would open the downtown doors each day—the cool old revolving doors and people would come through and sign in. For me, it was a whole new world. I was eighteen years old; I grew up in Raytown and I was surrounded by all of these beautiful women.

He remembers the Young Essentials Shop (YES Shop) as an attempt to appeal to the younger set. "Harzfeld's was a victim of an aging clientele… they were trying to find a younger, more vibrant clientele."

Roy would maintain, buy and ship supplies for the stores. He saw the evolution from the familiar green and white striped packaging to the new gray and burgundy color scheme. He also helped to liquidate store inventory and fixtures and shut down the warehouse when the time came. After the closing of the downtown store, he reminisced about the Benton mural: "I remember them coming in to box it up…they came in and built a superstructure with scaffolding to remove and crate it."

Later on, Roy was offered a job with Bonwit Teller but instead took a position as purchasing agent for Ann Taylor in Connecticut.

When asked about his thoughts relating to the decline of the specialty store, he answered, "There were a lot more retail choices—while people still shopped at Harzfeld's, it was more like a mission; a special occasion."

THE MONTGOMERY FAMILY, AS TOLD BY BETH ROBINSON

Adalyn Montgomery was my great-grandmother, who worked for Harzfeld's from at least 1930 until she retired. She worked in women's sportswear, the Gadabout Shop. Phoebe (Peggy) Young was Adalyn's sister, and she worked in the glove department. They both worked there long enough to become members of the Twenty-five-Year Club.

I had Harzfeld's clothes all while growing up. I was very well dressed. It was really quite something to tell someone you worked at Harzfeld's.

Dr. Penny Montgomery (Beth's mother) recounts visiting the store as a child:

I was practically raised at Harzfeld's. As you went in the door, a department on the right was the glove department. It was a long counter with plaster of Paris or wood hand models on stands. People would go there and sit on little stools to be fitted. They had a ton of those little drawers that held gloves. Right across from there was the hat department. Hats and gloves were all the rage. Farther down was the perfume counter…you always had the aroma. It's such an integral part of my childhood and my history.

Adalyn Montgomery (left) and her sister, Phoebe Young (right). Twenty-five-year pins and 7.5" x 5.5" watercolor portraits from 1945.

My father (Vernon Leroy Montgomery) worked there as an elevator boy in his teens, running the little wheel. Then my mother (Mary Jane Montgomery) was in alterations on the Plaza and became manager of the department. When Metcalf South opened, she became head of alterations there. We used to go to the rooftop at the store to watch the lights being lit for Christmas on the Plaza. Also, we would go to the upper floor of the downtown store to watch the American Royal parade.

[Regarding customer service,] *I remember my grandmother and her sister had books with five- by seven-inch pages in them; every customer had a page or two, or even five, in that book. They knew their families; they knew their likes and dislikes. It was a highly personalized shopping experience.*[81]

Notes

Chapter 1

1. Lester Siegel Jr., History of Harzfeld's, document.
2. *Kansas City Star*, "The Parisian Opening," February 25, 1891.
3. 1870 Census.
4. *Chicago Daily Tribune*, "A Cloak Collapse," September 20, 1884.
5. *Chicago Daily Tribune*, "Suicide of Albert Harzfeld," May 16, 1890.
6. *Kansas City Times*, "Petticoat Lane," December 8, 1921.
7. Henry C. Haskell Jr. and Richard B. Fowler (illustrations by Frank H. Miller), *City of the Future, A Narrative History of Kansas City, 1850–1950* (Kansas City, MO: Frank Glenn Publishing Co., Inc., 1950).
8. *'Mongst Us* (a revival of an earlier company newsletter by the same name, published by the Harzfeld's credit union) 1, no. 1., October 1940.
9. *Kansas City Star*, "Relive a Wedding Day," February 6, 1944.
10. *Kansas City Star*, "A Cloak Store's Success," October 7, 1906.

Chapter 2

11. *'Mongst Us* 1, no. 1, October 1940.
12. *Kansas City Star*, "Amateur Baseball Notes," May 1907–November 1909.
13. Frank Graham Jr., *Casey Stengel: His Half-Century in Baseball*, (New York: John Day Company, 1958).
14. Ibid.

15. *Time*, "In Kansas City," December 11, 1933.
16. *Kansas City Star*, "Seat Sale for Sunday 'Pop,'" March 3, 1915.
17. *Future*, April 12, 1935.

CHAPTER 3

18. *Kansas City Star*, "The New Parisian Ready," November 30, 1913.
19. *A Memorial and Biographical Record of Kansas City, Mo.*, 1896.
20. Ibid.
21. *Kansas City Star*, "The New Parisian Ready," November 30, 1913.
22. *Kansas City Star*, "Beauty's New Home," June 24, 1914.
23. Petticoat Lane Exhibit (online, closed), Kansas City Public Library.

CHAPTER 4

24. Richard B. Fowler, *Kansas City Star*, "Leaders in our Town," June 11, 1950.
25. *'Mongst Us* 1, no. 2, November 1940.
26. Ibid. 6, no. 2, April 1929.
27. Ibid. 6, no. 3, May 1929.
28. Ibid. 6, no. 4, June 1929.
29. *Kansas City Star*, September 27, 1926.
30. *The Country Club District*, J.C. Nichols Company promotional booklet, 1954.
31. *'Mongst Us* 2, no. 4, June 1942.
32. Fifty-fifth-anniversary company publication, 1946.

CHAPTER 5

33. Thomas Hart Benton, *An Artist in America* (revised edition) (Lawrence: University of Kansas Press, Twayne Publishers, 1951).
34. Thomas Hart Benton, *This is the Legend of "Achelous and Hercules" as told by Thomas H. Benton*, from small folding flyer given to customers of Harzfeld's, 1947.
35. Interview with Lester Siegel Jr., September 2009.
36. *Kansas City Times*, June 3, 1978.

CHAPTER 6

37. *Kansas City Star*, "The New Parisian Ready," November 30, 1913.
38. *Boxoffice Showmandiser*, October 27, 1945.
39. Ibid., April 5, 1947.
40. John McElwee, *Greenbriar Picture Shows*, greenbriarpictureshows.blogspot.com.
41. *Independent*, March 31, 1979.
42. *Petticoat Laner*, company publication, December 1952.
43. *California Stylist*, April 1956.

CHAPTER 7

44. *Christian Science Monitor*, April 23, 1954.
45. *Petticoat Laner*, company publication, April 1954.
46. Recollections sent via e-mail from Wendy Newhouse Hadgden, January 2009.
47. *Petticoat Laner*, company publication, February 1956.

CHAPTER 8

48. *Town Pictorial*, February 27, 1948.
49. *Daily Capital News* (Jefferson City, MO), "Negros [*sic*] Boycott Five KC Stores," December 19, 1958.
50. *Kansas City Times*, January 20, 1961.
51. Harry S Truman Papers, Harry S Truman Library and Museum. Letter from Lester Siegel Sr., May 1, 1961.
52. Judy Ancel, *The Garment Workers* (Talk for Kansas City Labor History Tour), Institute for Labor Studies, October 17, 24, 1992.

CHAPTER 9

53. Interview with Lester Siegel Jr., September 2009.
54. *Kansas City Star*, "Lester Siegel Jr. to Harzfeld's Post," January 30, 1966.
55. Interview with Lorene Roberson, June 2009.
56. *Kansas City Star*, August 2, 1967.
57. Jim Williams oral history interview with Elizabeth Safly for the Harry S Truman National Historic Site, August 15–16, 1990.

58. *Washington Post*, February 6, 1972.

59. *New York Times*, March 15, 1959.

60. *Washington Post*, October 31, 1974.

61. John Brooks Walton, *One Hundred More Historic Tulsa Homes* (Tulsa, OK: HCE Publications, the Tulsa Foundation for Architecture, 2001).

62. Jason Ashley Wright, *Tulsa World*, June 17, 2009.

63. *Historic Kansas City News*, published by Historic Kansas City Foundation, August 1977.

64. *Kansas City Times*, June 3, 1978.

65. *Kansas City Star*, "Ms. Stegner Takes Harzfeld's Reins," October 4, 1978.

66. *New York Times*, February 15, 1980.

67. Jerry Knight, *Washington Post*, November 11, 1981.

CHAPTER 10

68. John Rothchild, *Going for Broke: How Robert Campeau Bankrupted the Retail Industry, Jolted the Junk Bond Market, and Brought the Booming Eighties to a Crashing Halt* (New York: Simon & Schuster, 1991).

69. Jennifer Mann Fuller, *Kansas City Star*, March 1990.

CHAPTER 11

70. Interview with Arthur III and Gary Kabrick, July 28, 2009.

71. *'Mongst Us* 1, no. 6, March 1941.

72. Interview with Warren Dalton, May 2, 2009.

73. Recollections sent via e-mail from Judy Mendelsohn Lanes, August 2009.

74. Recollections sent via e-mail from JoLynne (Walz) Martinez, January 2008.

75. Recollections sent via e-mail from Lloyd Hellman, August 2009.

76. Phone interview with Drolette (Bradley) Weideman, September 2009.

77. Story provided by Mary Jane Krugh, September 2009.

78. Recollections sent via e-mail from John G. Cate, March 2009.

79. Recollections sent via e-mail from Dr. Deborah Stephens, October 2008.

80. Story provided by Lorene Roberson, June 2009.

81. Interview with Dr. Penny Montgomery and Beth Robinson, July 2009.

About the Authors

Joe and Michele Boeckholt are both practicing graphic designers living and working in the Kansas City metro area. Originally from Iowa, they met at Iowa State University in a foundations drawing class, and relocated to Kansas City after graduating from the College of Art and Design.

Joe and Michele share an appreciation for local history, popular culture and the visual arts. The pair can be found exploring the city's antique shops, flea markets and other collectible outlets. In fact, a flea market is where the genesis ephemera was discovered related to the personal project that's evolved into *Harzfeld's: A Brief History*.

Joe currently shares a position of creative director in Rockhurst University's public relations and marketing office. Michele has been the manager of graphic design at the Nelson-Atkins Museum of Art for ten years. In the fall of 2003, they mounted a Harzfeld's exhibition at the Johnson County Central Resource Library.

Visit us at
www.historypress.net